WESTMAR COLLEGE LIBRARY

P9-CTQ-594

INTERNATIONAL TEXTBOOKS IN ART EDUCATION

Italo L. de Francesco, Consulting Editor

Student Teaching In Art

Student Teaching In Art

A Handbook for Student Teachers
and Beginning Art Teachers

WELLINGTON B. GRAY

Director, Department of Art,
East Carolina College

INTERNATIONAL TEXTBOOK COMPANY

Scranton, Pennsylvania

707
G7833

N
87
.G68

53320

Copyright ©, 1960, by International Textbook Company. All rights reserved. Printed in the United States of America. Library of Congress Catalog Card Number: 60-9018.

To Norma, Dr. De, and students – past and present – without whose help and inspiration there would not have been the incentive to teach.

Editor's Preface

Student teaching, whether in art or in other subject fields, is the summation of the process of preparing a teacher. It is also "the proof of the pudding."

It is the summation of the entire period of preparation in that now the prospective teacher will try his wings. He will attempt to put into practice what he has learned in psychology and method in his own teaching. The nature of pupils, their interests, their capacities, and their aptitudes are now considered in an integrated manner toward the ultimate end—to teach effectively.

How valid is the methodology? How well does the prospective teacher know his field? How effective are his methods? Is he capable of integrated thinking—planning—teaching? In short, how good a teacher is he? That's the proof of it all.

Art education, in addition to encountering problems common to all teaching, holds a further challenge for the novice, namely, the understanding of the creative process. Facts are facts, mathematical formulae are fixed, grammar changes very slowly, but creative unfolding is a unique problem with each pupil, each time he undertakes to create.

Therefore, STUDENT TEACHING IN ART, as presented by Dr. Gray, includes all facets of teaching; he is not indifferent to the *practical aspects* of running a good classroom. Oftener than not, it is the "little things" which annoy young teachers; they seem removed from his major interest, even unnecessary. Yet, they are necessary checks in school situations, and young teachers ought to be aware of them.

In this volume, Dr. Gray is rendering a much needed professional service to art education at a time when excellence of performance is the keynote to both teaching and learning.

Italo L. de Francesco

To The Student Teacher

This Handbook is the result of a felt need on the part of many student teachers, master teachers in art education programs, and college professors who supervise in this area of teacher education.

The present work offers a positive approach by suggesting actions which can be taken by the student teachers. They are based on the experiences of former student teachers, master teachers, experienced art teachers, and professors.

The contents include types of successful methodology, relations with the master teacher and other personnel, management of the classroom, the process of planning for teaching, and the evaluation of the results of teaching. Procedures for securing the first teaching position, memberships in professional art and educational organizations, the continual professional and creative growth necessary for the art teacher, and a statement of professional ethics are also covered.

While this Handbook is not all-inclusive, it is intended as a ready reference for the novice, to suggest courses of action and to furnish some answers to questions which most student teachers seem to ask. It is hoped that the material will be of real value to you and that the information will permit you to enjoy the experience of working with children for the first time.

W. B. GRAY

Acknowledgments

No book can be the exclusive effort of the author. There are many others who share in the success of the author. For the assistance received in planning and writing this book and for photographs, I am indebted to many people.

During the past ten years, student teachers in art from the University of Illinois, the School of the Art Institute of Chicago, State Teachers College at Edinboro, Penna., and East Carolina College at Greenville, N. C. have helped in many ways, particularly in stating problems and in offering solutions. My thanks to all of them for sharing their experiences with me.

Supervisors of student teaching, cooperating teachers, and administrators have also been generous with their counsel and confidence. Dr. L. H. Van Laningham, Director of Student Teaching at Edinboro State Teachers College; Professor Harold Schultz of the University of Illinois; Dr. J. L. Oppelt, Director of Student Teaching at East Carolina College; Miss Laura Boice, Art Supervisor at Rocky Mount, N. C.; Mrs. Norma W. Gray, Art Supervisor of Greenville, N. C.; and Dr. Sherrick Fisher of San Diego State College are among these professional friends.

Dr. Edgar Hirshberg and Mrs. Norma W. Gray read the typescript and offered significant criticism and help with the manuscript.

Above all, my thanks to Dr. I. L. de Francesco, President, State Teachers College, Kutztown, Penna., without whose professional and personal encouragement and interest I should not have started my professional career nor have written a book.

Finally, my sincere appreciation to all who have granted permission to quote from the sources indicated.

W. B. G.

Contents

Student Teaching In Art

Student Teaching Is Important

THE student teacher generally asks a most basic question, Why student teaching? The answer to this question is simple enough although the process involved may be quite complicated: to give you experience. Because of the far-reaching influence which the teacher has on the lives of the children he teaches, he must have some prior experience in the teaching processes, under guidance, before he accepts a regular teaching position. In fact, most states in the United States will not give a prospective teacher a license to teach—a teaching certificate—until he has had some practice in the art and science of guiding children.

Introduction to Your Career

Student teaching, or cadet teaching as it is sometimes called, is an immensely important part of the college education of the future teacher. Most men would not go to an inexperienced barber. No one would employ an office worker to build a house just because he owns a hammer and a saw. What an employer wants is someone in whom he can place confidence, someone with experience. With graduation from college and the subsequent teaching certificate from the state education department, one can at least say that the applicant has had some experience and is qualified to begin teaching on his own.

Student teaching also gives the future teacher an opportunity to work with a master teacher and to observe how such an experienced individual handles the various problems arising in the classroom. In the art class this is particularly important because there will be twenty different problems if there are twenty students in the class. Each of these problems will have to be solved separately and, quite possibly, in different ways.

Period of Experimentation

One quarter or one semester will not give you as much experience in student teaching as you suspect. Nor will it make you an ultimate authority. In fact, if you are like the average student teacher, you will soon realize

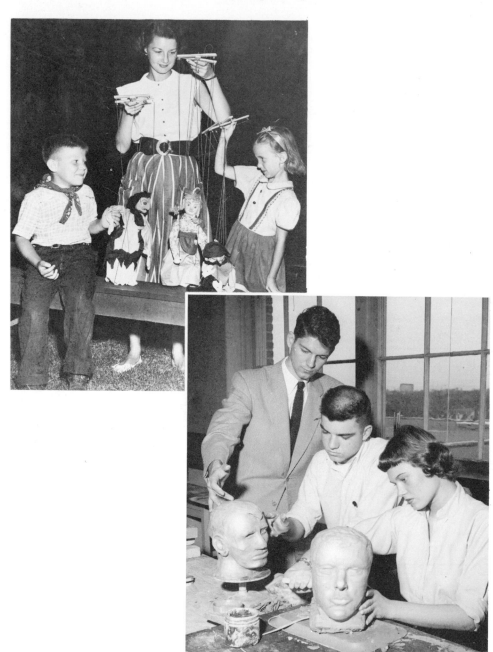

Student teaching provides a period of time for the beginning teacher to experiment with teaching methods and devices. Experimentation will indicate appropriate learning experiences, adequate teaching techniques, and progressive aesthetic development of the child.

just how little you really do know. You will come to see that there is much more that you will have to assimilate in order to really deserve the title "Teacher." You will find that fine methods and excellent theories and philosophies need intelligent interpretations and sound applications. These interpretations and applications come with continuous study within the classroom proper, with actual teaching under guidance, and with observation of master teachers in action.

The initial few weeks of student teaching are really planned so as to give you an opportunity to experiment in several different areas of subject matter in a limited manner under the guidance of the master teacher. You may present lessons or units to the classes which you teach in a variety of ways so that you will learn by experience which is the best way for you to present the types of art experiences with which you experiment.

Not only will you have an opportunity to experiment with methods of presentation, but you will also be able to experiment with materials, techniques, and tools. Quite often you will find that you will be confronted with tools, materials, or techniques with which you are totally unfamiliar. You will have to experiment by yourself as well as with your students in class.

Learning Routines

There are other aspects of the total job of teaching which the student teacher will encounter in terms of practical experience. These aspects come under the heading of routines. You may be required to maintain the attendance register, to supervise extracurricular activities, to assign marks to student projects, to participate in faculty meetings, to work on faculty committees, or to work with individual teachers. Some of these duties you will have, if you are employed as an art teacher, others if you are employed as an art supervisor.

ATTENDANCE REGISTER. Should you be employed as an art teacher you will have to keep the attendance records of your students. This is particularly true if you have a "home room." You must realize that all states tend to account for pupil attendance in different ways. In some states the attendance register is known as a "state register"; this means that the attendance records are to be maintained on forms or in a book provided by the state department of education. Some of these forms, as in the case of Pennsylvania, are quite complicated.

In some states the classroom teacher turns in local forms to the office, and the school administrator takes care of the submission of state forms to the state department of education.

SUPERVISION OF EXTRACURRICULAR ACTIVITIES. The number of so-called extracurricular activities, those student-centered, school-oriented activities usually scheduled outside the regular school day, varies from school to school. Some activities in communities which are basically rural in nature are scheduled during the regular school day. This situation prevails where students have to travel long distances by bus. Of course there are some activities, such as dances, which are usually scheduled at night regardless of the location of the school.

Quite often the art teacher is called on to help sponsor the school year-book, to sponsor the art club, to help with posters, to help sponsor activities of the Junior Red Cross, or to assist with stage productions. These are activities which are art-related.

Of course there are programs and activities which are not art-related but which you will be called upon to supervise and/or sponsor. The author was once required to take tickets at home football games while one of his associates was responsible for maintaining order at home basketball games in another school. Most teachers are requested to chaperone dances on occasion. Some-times the chaperones are also asked to supervise the decorations, the refresh-ments, the programs, the hiring of the dance orchestra, and so forth. These responsibilities vary with the location of the school and the philosophy of the principal or the superintendent, but it is very likely that you will be asked to help with the extracurricular program.

REPORTING PUPIL PROGRESS AND EVALUATION. Evaluation of student work indicates in this context the assignment of a grade for the creative efforts of students. Cumulatively, the grades are then reported to the parent through the use of report cards, letters, personal visits, etc. Varying philosophies of report-ing pupil progress are to be found in different schools.

In awarding a "grade" to a student, some schools use an alphabet sys-tem—A, B, C, etc. Other schools use a numerical system—1, 2, 3, etc. The author was once employed in a school system where all grades were to be reported on a percentage basis. It was perplexing to see an art teacher assign one student a 74% on a drawing which was not a "passing" grade, and to award another student in the same class a 75% on his drawing, the latter being a passing grade. It should be apparent that you should learn the grading system in use in the school in which you do your student teaching.

In addition to learning the grading system you must learn about the total evaluation of a student in terms of promotion policy. As is true with grades, there are differing philosophies of promotion policy in operation in various schools.

Automatic, or social promotion as it is often called, is one kind of advancement in school quite popular in some districts. This philosophy is based on the chronological age of the pupil and the belief that he will be a better adjusted individual if he is promoted annually with children of his own age group.

Adequate planning by student teacher insures an excellent climate for learning. Children will use their imaginations and experiment in using materials and techniques.

Regular promotion from grade to grade is based on the students' successful completion of required work. Perhaps the important term of this statement is the word successful. This means that the idea of quality has been introduced. In order to be promoted from one grade to the next succeeding higher grade, the student must meet the minimum performance standards in the various school areas. While you will probably have little to say about the promotion of the child, it is important for you to understand the philosophy of grading and promotion so that you cope intelligently with individual students whom you find in your classes.

You must learn how much value in assigning a grade or determining a promotion is placed on the effort expended by the individual student to achieve desired goals. Some students place a high value on effort expended by the student. However, there are many school districts which will consider no criteria except quality in performance.

More will be mentioned about evaluation in Chapter 5, *Planning For Teaching,* and Chapter 8, *Aspects of Evaluation.*

FACULTY MEETINGS. Faculty meetings are a necessity in the teaching profession. They are needed and used for several purposes, among them to clarify administrative details and to determine educational programs.[1] Usually the teachers' meetings are regularly scheduled on an average of once a month. There are many scheduling plans for faculty meetings in terms of the time. Youch lists six plans for the timing of the faculty meeting:[2]

1. Before school in the morning
2. During the noon hour
3. Dinner or supper meetings
4. Evening meetings
5. Saturday or Sunday meetings
6. During the regular school day

Your interest and participation in the scheduled faculty meetings will give you an insight and understanding of the administrative and philosophical structure of the school in which you do your student teaching. Your participation will probably be on an inactive basis during the time you are assigned as a student teacher, and you will have no professional status or voice in the meetings. However, the faculty meeting is one of the routine matters with which you must become familiar in order to understand how decisions are reached and how the professional staff is administered. When you become a full member of the profession you should then participate actively by voicing your feelings when appropriate and by voting on issues that arise.

[1] W. A. Youch, M. H. Bartels and E. Morris, *The Beginning Teacher* (New York: Henry Holt & Co., Inc., 1955), pp. 226-229.
[2] *Loc. cit.*

COMMITTEES AND INDIVIDUALS. As a student teacher you will probably not have membership on faculty committees. Most of the time, however, you may be invited to sit in on committee meetings. In this way you will learn committee procedures and the importance of such committees to the teaching staff. Quite often you will find faculty committees working on problems of curriculum, faculty welfare, athletics, discipline, assemblies, and so forth. Many times, when you have become a regular member of a faculty, you will find it necessary to belong to such committees or at least to cooperate with them. Whenever you have the opportunity of observing the workings of a teachers committee, take advantage of the opportunity for future use.

Even as a student teacher you will find opportunities for cooperating with other teachers on the staff. Often you will find that things which come up in your classes will be of importance to the work of other teachers in the school, especially where the children are concerned.

Recently a student teacher from a Southern college was working in a large city junior high school. She found a student in her art class who seemed most interested in what was going on, who was doing an excellent job, but who was keeping pretty well to himself. She found out, by consulting the student's home-room teacher, that the student was a failure in school. The art class was the only time during the day when he was happy, productive, and, above all, a success. By cooperating with another teacher and consulting with her, the student teacher was most effective in changing the attitude and probably the life of a potential troublemaker. Granted, all of the cases are not as striking as this example. But it does illustrate the necessity of cooperation in routine investigations and inquiries in order to be an effective teacher.

Summary

In this chapter we have considered three reasons for the importance of student teaching. The three reasons stated for this importance are: 1) it is an introduction to your teaching career; 2) it is a period of experimentation in method, techniques, tools, and materials; 3) it is an opportunity to learn something of the routines and associations existing within the school.

Another main reason, not mentioned because it has little immediate relationship to the student teacher, is that the major accreditation group, the National Council for the Accreditation of Teacher Education, requires student teaching as a prerequisite for regional accreditation. This means that if a college educating young people for the teaching profession wishes to be on the accredited list of colleges in this field it will require its students to spend some time in student teaching.

Beyond all these reasons, however, there is the opportunity to associate with children and to apply what has been learned in college classes. Never truer is the axiom, "learn by doing."

For Further Thinking and Doing

1. What do you expect to get out of student teaching? Of teaching as a career?
2. As a beginning teacher take stock of yourself. What are your strengths? Weaknesses?
3. What emotions and attitudes do you have as you begin your student teaching? Why do you think you have these?

Your Philosophy of Art Education

To be sure, each of us has ideas and ideals by which we live. These are the beliefs that make the daily job of living an important matter. Another word for belief could be philosophy. What do you believe in when it comes to art education? What is your philosophy?

It is important to you as a young, beginning teacher to develop a statement of philosophy of your chosen profession as early as you can in your career. Undoubtedly you have begun a collection of ideas in the studio and in the lecture hall which have become beliefs. During your apprenticeship in student teaching you will probably develop more ideas and consolidate still others. These ideas and ideals have probably been based, to a large degree, on the experience of others whom you know, through professional readings for college courses, or from authorities who are considered reliable in the field of art education. What they have learned by their experience, what they have written concerning their experience, investigations, and studies, and probably your own limited experience, have more than likely crystalized some of your beliefs into a philosophy, whether you realize it or not.

Many statements have been made as to the goal of the art education program in the public schools. These statements range from the most complete to the most obvious. Some of the more readily accepted objectives of the art program are stated below. It must be mentioned that these are not all the goals which could be listed as they are worded more or less in broad terms. Each individual community will have different needs and, therefore, different objectives for the art program. It must be further realized that the goals are not listed in order of importance or preference. The individual situation will place more emphasis on one than on another objective, depending on the community, the breadth of art preparation of the teachers involved, and the general taste which the particular community has developed over the years. Any statement of your philosophy of art education should contain some reference to your beliefs concerning the following goals:

1. Aesthetic development of the child
2. Expression through art education

3. Good citizenship and the art program
4. Mental and creative potentialities of the child

Aesthetic Development of the Child

Basically, most recognized authorities consider that a very important goal of an art program, at any level of instruction, is the aesthetic development of the student. The art teacher must realize that only a small percentage of his art students will be producers of art on a professional basis. It should certainly be apparent, therefore, that a majority of the students in art classes need an expressive rather than a technical approach. This approach can be developed in many ways—from the laboratory situation to the art history and appreciation type of presentation. What is of the utmost importance is the realization on the part of the art teacher that he is dealing primarily with consumers of art products rather than with producers. It is imperative that the teacher give the boys and girls a basic understanding of many art fields so that they may become intelligent consumers, capable of appreciating the arts, and thereby developing aesthetic taste and judgement.

Each student and future citizen will eventually purchase his own clothing, will probably buy some form of transportation, and will undoubtedly purchase furniture, furnishings, and perhaps even a home. Is it not reasonable then to teach the student something about color, design, proportion, texture, and other elements and principles of design when all products are dependent to some degree, on these principles and elements for sales? A large percentage of automobiles today are purchased on the basis of appearance. In recent years, textures have become important items of consideration in products, due to newer processes and materials. One may conclude, therefore, that the development of the appreciative aspects of the visual and plastic arts is deserving of strong emphasis in any art program.

Expression Through Art Education[1]

Another major objective of any art program probably should be that of expression. It is believed by most art educators that a child should be permitted as many different materials as possible, dependent, of course, on the child's ability to handle the specific materials. Obviously enamelling on copper is not a particularly appropriate activity for a first grade student. In an experience-oriented program a pupil becomes conversant with the potentialities and limitations of materials and may develop such an interest in a particular medium that he begins to think in terms of the vocational possibilities which this medium pos-

[1] Ernest Ziegfeld, *Art in the College Program of General Education* (New York: Teachers College, Bureau of Publications, Columbia University, 1953), pp. 149-150.

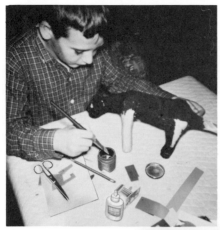

Children should be permitted as many art materials as possible according to their ability to handle them. Such a program will enable the student to develop mentally, physically, and creatively.

sesses. Experimentation with many kinds of materials can and should, in the earlier age groups, develop coordination and muscular control. Such development is inherent in the use of clay and plasticene as well as in many drawing and painting media. Experimentation with a variety of materials and processes not only strengthens the appreciative aspects of the program but also opens up vistas of vocational possibilities in the various visual and plastic arts.

Good Citizenship Through Art

Good citizenship is an important consideration and a major goal in an art education program or in any program of studies. Perhaps, because art is a matter of personal vision and because in art education it is possible to respect the abilities and purposes of individual students, there is more opportunity to develop good citizenship through art than in many other fields. The atmosphere of the art laboratory offers a challenge for the practice of democratic action in the planning and execution or work on the part of the teachers as well as students. Cooperative effort and team play on the part of students and teachers alike are possible in many directions—learning to consider the rights of others, group interaction, recognition of authority, and respect for property. By practicing these aspects of good citizenship constantly, art teaches democratic principles by example rather than by precept.

Creative Potential

Ziegfeld[2] points out that fostering the growth of the creative potential of each child, as well as the stimulation of his mental capacities, is one of the important objectives of a good art program. Each individual strives to express himself in some way. The art program should be the curricular area in which the student can express himself and relate himself, his ideas, and his experiences in his own way. Thus he will develop his imagination, ability to think, and personal judgment. Judgement of the child and his accomplishments on a scale of adult standards is unfair to the child, for he has not lived long enough to acquire all that is bad in the civilization in which he finds himself. Lowenfeld examines some of the interferences which do much to detour the creative growth of the child. He says, "What civilization has buried we must try to regain by recreating the natural base necessary for such free creation."[3]

The four objectives cited above-could be called a philosophy of art education. The profession has traveled a long way to reach such a philosophy.

[2] *Ibid.,* pp. 146-149.
[3] Viktor Lowenfeld, *Creative and Mental Growth* (3d ed.; New York: The Macmillan Co., 1957)

One of the tenets of the workable philosophy of art education is the aesthetic development of the child. One way in which this is accomplished is to involve the child in creative activity.

Philosophies have changed over the years since art education first became a part of the curriculum. Art education, as a regular subject in the curriculum, is a recent addition. One must have an understanding of the background of the field and of the journey so far in order to have some idea of the future of art education.

Some art educators may feel that our area of the school program of instruction is the most important part of the student's life. However, only eighty years ago our field was represented as a regular subject of the school curriculum in only a very few schools in the United States.

Historical Considerations of Philosophies

During the time that art education has been developing into a full-fledged subject in the curriculum, it has undergone many different emphases and changes. You have probably discussed in art education classes these varying emphases and changes. Table I indicates chronologically the several major movements which have come on the scene in past years.

Early attempts to establish art education in the schools were spotty and were tried in different sections of the country. They ranged from the early advocacy of Benjamin Franklin in his *Proposed Hints for an Academy*[4] to the introduction of art as a subject in the curriculum in Syracuse, New York, in 1870.

Over the years art education has been influenced strongly by the purposes of professional educators and psychologists. The influence of such men as Froebel, Pestalozzi, Herbart, Mann, Dewey, Kilpatrick, Thorndike, and others has been felt in the area of art education as it has been felt in other curricular areas.

And of course the influence of professional art educators has been of the greatest importance through the years. Such leaders as Dow, Whitford, Winslow, Kirby, Klar, Mathias, Tannahill, Ziegfeld, Gaitskell, D'Amico, Landis, and de Francesco must be reckoned with as artists and educators whose leadership has done most of the literature, methodology, and philosophy of art education.

Whitford, an early chronicler of art education history, states the several slogans which are indicative of the influences in art education. He states them as "Art for Art's Sake," "Art for Industry," and "Art for Life's Sake."[5]

Current Considerations of Philosophy

Because of the movements, emphases, and influences, and the art teachers who were educated under such guidance, there arose in the areas of art and art education a great deal of controversy and confusion. Munro has this to say: "One result of controversy and confusion in the world of art has been to produce a spirit of vagueness and uncertainty in art education. . . . Hampered by far reaching dissension in its own field, it has had to feel its way and struggle for a definite place in the school and college curriculum."[6]

[4] Italo L. de Francesco, *Art Education, Its Means and Ends* (New York: Harper & Brothers, 1958), p. 62.

[5] William Whitford, *An Introduction to Art Education* (New York: D. Appleton-Century Co., 1937), p. 3.

[6] Thomas Munro, *Art Education, Its Philosophy and Psychology* (New York: The Liberal Arts Press, Inc., 1956), p. 44.

TABLE I

T IME, M OVEMENT, AND L EADERS OF A RT E DUCATION IN THE U NITED S TATES

Time*	Emphasis and/or Influences	Leaders
1815	Individual efforts to teach art to children	
1821	Experimental introduction into Massachusetts schools	W. B. Fowle
1835	Applied design influence	
1840-on	Local interest in school art: Philadelphia, Baltimore, Cleveland, Washington, and so forth	R. Peale, Mann, Brainerd
1850	Froebelian influence	
1860	Massachusetts school drawing on state basis	W. Smith
1865	Art teacher education begun in Syracuse	W. T. Harris
1873	Massachusetts School of Art founded	W. Smith
1876	"Art for Industry," Philadelphia Centennial	
1881	Herbartian influence	MacMurray
1893	Hegelian influence—General Education	Harper
1895	Art as Experience	Dewey
1898	General appreciation influence—Art by rule	Dow
1904	"Art for Life's Sake"	Sargent
1907	Industrial arts emphasis	Whitford
1915-on	Creativity and integration	Cizek, Winslow
1927	Art for all children	D'Amico
1932	The child artist	Dix
1937	Art for living	Faulkner, Ziegfeld
1945	Reemphasis of general education	Landis, Ziegfeld
1948	Art as education for growth and development	Lowenfeld
1949	National organization for art, NAEA	De Francesco, Ziegfeld
1955	International organization for art	Ziegfeld

* Time-dates indicate an approximation in most cases.

The dissension referred to by Munro has resulted in what de Francesco calls the four "current emphases in art education."[7] These four emphases indicate the current position of art education in relation to its philosophy. Briefly stated they are as follows:

    1. "Creative growth is merely one facet of total child growth."[8] Viktor Lowenfeld, in his work *Creative and Mental Growth*,[9] has become the

---

[7] Italo L. de Francesco, "Experience as Basis for Creative Growth" *This Is Art Education, 1952* (Kutztown: National Art Education Association), pp. 130-132.

[8] *Ibid.*

[9] Viktor Lowenfeld, *Creative and Mental Growth,* 3d ed.; New York: The Macmillan Co., 1957.

leading proponent of this particular emphasis. He has combined unique insights into the psychology of learning and art education by classifying children as to type. He indicates that children should be allowed to develop according to their personality types. He also classifies stages of growth in terms of the visual products of children.

2. The second emphasis indicates that "creative activity is an autonomous operation based upon sensuous, creative, and 'visual thinking'."[10] This point of view signifies that creation by means of visual forms is one of man's natural attributes. One of the focal points of such an emphasis is that the child must find and establish his own approach to the creative. This means experimentation. "The fact that children vary in the media they prefer to use leads to the recommendation that as many different materials as possible should be placed at their disposal."[11]

3. The third approach recognizes the urge to create as something as natural as breathing. But this naturalness needs to be fed continually by constant experimentation or examination of materials, tools, techniques, and ideas. While experimentation is important to the second point of view above, the experimentation here is for a different purpose. Here the emphasis is on the art experience being the development of "social literacy" suggested by systematic learnings.

4. The final point of view indicates the relationships of creative abilities and life-centered activities. Perhaps, integration or core learnings would be key words here since both types of programs deal with common areas of living and the concurrent learnings which take place in several areas, art being but one of them.

Having stated the four points of view of art education today, de Francesco then proceeded to indicate seven art activity areas based on different types of experience as implementation for a program.[12] Briefly stated these types of experiences are:

1. Self-centered experience
2. Materials-centered and tools-centered experience
3. Life of enjoyment experiences
4. Independent work experiences
5. Experimentation-centered experience
6. Social values-centered experience
7. Problem solving experience

[10] De Francesco, *op. cit.,* p. 131.
[11] Charles D. Gaitskell, *Children and Their Art* (New York: Harcourt, Brace & Co., 1958),
p. 47.
[12] De Francesco, *op. cit.,* pp. 133-136.

One prime consideration in dealing with the philosophy of art education in the United States is the perpetuation of democracy. Lowenfeld emphasizes the point of view that freedom of expression, especially in art education, is necessary for a democratic society. He states: "In order to develop in the child this freedom of expression essential for a democratic society, it is then necessary that the teacher studies and identifies himself with:

1. The child at the different levels of growth
2. The subject matter with which the child deals
3. The social environment in which the child lives
4. The means of expression of the child."[13]

"Democracy can survive only if its educational philosophy is consonant with freedom of thought and action. Art education for our time can best serve the children and the nation by adopting procedures and methods that do not impose and direct but rather encourage and stimulate."[14] While this is getting close to methodology in teaching, it stresses the point that democratic principles in a philosophy of art education are a necessity.

Summary

In this chapter some of the requisites for a philosophy of art and art education have been given. These requisites were stated as the aesthetic development of the child, expression through art education, good citizenship, and training the mental and creative potentialities of the child.

There followed a brief statement of the historical developments in the area of art education and a section dealing with some of the contemporary approaches to art education philosophy.

The art program today is a far cry from what it was 100 years ago. From the concept of geometric, correctly outlined, and carefully rendered light and shade drawing to the kinds of drawing and painting, commercial and applied arts, and the crafts fields of today, from a concept of teaching art to further other knowledge to the kind of art teaching which takes into account experimentation, aesthetic development, citizenship, and mental and creative growth is a mighty big step. The place of the teacher in the art program has changed from the "special teacher" to that of the "resource" faculty member. Currently the trend, curriculumwise, is in terms of a child-centered, experience-oriented program. Changes are constantly being made in the philosophy of our curricular area. This is as it should be since change usually indicates growth and development. Only time will tell what the future holds for the art program in our country.

---

[13] Viktor Lowenfeld, "The Meaning of Art Education in a Democracy," *This is Art Education, 1952* (Kutztown: National Art Education Association), p. 79.

[14] Italo L. de Francesco, Editors Preface, *This is Art Education, 1952* (Kutztown: National Art Education Association).

For Further Reading

Brameld, Theodore, *Patterns of Educational Philosophy*, New York: World Book Co., 1950.

De Francesco, Italo L., *Art Education, Its Means and Ends*, New York: Harper & Brothers, 1958.

————, "Experience as Basis for Creative Growth," *This Is Art Education, 1952*, Kutztown: National Art Education Association.

————, Editor's Preface, *This Is Art Education, 1952*, Kutztown: National Art Education Association.

Gaitskell, Charles D., *Children and Their Art*, New York: Harcourt, Brace and Co., 1958.

Keiler, Manfred, *Art In The Schoolroom*, Lincoln: University of Nebraska Press, 1951.

Logan, Frederick M., *Growth of Art in American Schools*, New York: Harper & Brothers, 1954.

Lowenfeld, Viktor, *Creative and Mental Growth*, 3d ed.; New York: The Macmillan Co., 1957.

————, "The Meaning of Art Education in a Democracy," *This Is Art Education, 1952*, Kutztown: National Art Education Association.

Mendelowitz, Daniel M., *Children Are Artists*, Stanford: Stanford University Press, 1954.

Munro, Thomas, *Art Education, Its Philosophy and Psychology*, New York: The Liberal Arts Press, Inc., 1956.

Whitford, William, *An Introduction to Art Education*, New York: D. Appleton-Century Co., 1937.

Ziegfeld, Ernest, *Art in the College Program of General Education*, New York: Teachers College, Bureau of Publications, Columbia University, 1953.

For Further Thinking and Doing

1. Determine the specific contributions of each of the following art educators: Dow, Whitford, Winslow, Kirby, Klar, Cole, Mathias, Tannahill, Ziegfeld, Gaitskell, D'Amico, Landis, Lowenfeld, and de Francesco.

2. How has the leadership of Froebel, Pestalozzi, Herbart, Mann, Dewey, Kilpatrick, Thorndike, and Dix affected art education?

3. Formulate your own philosophy of art education and put it on paper. From time to time during your tenure as a student art teacher compare your thinking with your statement.

3

Levels of Creative Development

THERE is probably no such thing as an "average" child. We achieve the ideal of the average child by lumping together the abilities of a specific group of children in any, and possibly all, areas of learning—the good and the bad, the slow and the fast. Psychologists have shown that one child will differ in a number of ways from any other child.

In public education we find children in school grouped by the age-grade formula. Because one can find many educators who indicate educational growth by specific grade numbers and still others who indicate such growth by chronological age, it is perhaps wiser to consider both ways of indicating educational growth. As a result we have what has become known as the age-grade formula.

We can find in any one class of children in school, as related specifically to art education, extremes in abilities of as much as one grade lower and one grade higher than that of the class designation. Or to put it another way, we will find children in any one grade in school who represent three different chronological age years in terms of creative growth.

Because children differ from individual to individual, you as an art teacher must know and be able to recognize the usual developmental sequence of creative ability. The several authorities in the field all pretty well agree on the specific definition of any particular stage of behavior patterns. But for reasons of their own, many have their own titles for the several stages. Table II lists five of these authorities and the titles they assign to each of the several levels of creative growth. You must realize that creative growth is but one of several different growth patterns through which the child progresses. It is almost a certainty that you have been given this kind of information in psychology classes before you have reached this point in your college career.

From reliable literature six creative maturation levels are presented for discussion. They are manipulation, presymbolic, symbolic, beginning realism, reasoning, and the adolescent stages. You must realize that every child in each grade will have reached one of these categories. For a specific grade level, some children will not have reached the norm for the grade while other children will

TABLE II
TITLES OF LEVELS OF CREATIVE GROWTH

Age	De Francesco[1]	Gaitskell[2]	Knudson and Christensen[3]	Landis[4]	Lowenfeld[5]
2-5 yrs	Manipulative Stage 1. Uncontrolled 2. Controlled 3. Named	Manipulation 1. Random 2. Controlled 3. Named	Scribbling	Manipulative	Scribbling 1. Without differentiation 2. Controlled 3. Circular 4. Named
gr K-1	Presymbolic Stage			Form Experimental	Pre-schematic
gr 2-3	Symbolic Stage	Symbols	Symbolic Stage	Early Expressive	Schematic
gr 4-5	Inceptive Realism	Pre-adolescent	Transition Stage		Dawning Realism
gr 6-7	Analytical Realism				Pseudorealism

[1] Italo L. de Francesco, *Art Education, Its Means and Ends* (New York: Harper & Brothers, 1958), pp. 249-268.
[2] Charles Gaitskell, *Children and Their Art* (New York: Harcourt, Brace & Co., 1958), pp. 129-142.
[3] E. H. Knudson, and E. M. Christensen, *Children's Art Education* (Peoria: Chas. A. Bennett Co., Inc., 1957), pp. 16-18.
[4] Mildred Landis, *Meaningful Art Education* (Peoria: Chas. A. Bennett Co., Inc., 1951), pp. 101-105.
[5] Viktor Lowenfeld, *Creative and Mental Growth* (3d ed.; New York: The Macmillan Co., 1957), pp. 86-255.

have surpassed the norm and will be working at a higher level of creative development.

Manipulative Stage

From about the age of two years on the child will manipulate various materials. That is to say that the child will explore the nature of the material rather than use it in an adult manner. Given a pencil or crayon the very young child will grasp it much the same as an older person would hold a hammer. The result will be marks made on a piece of paper called "scribbles." In the same manner if he is using clay, the child will squeeze the clay through his fingers in an uncontrolled manner. If the child has paint and brushes at this age level, he will poke the brush at the paper, the result being a continuation of the use of the pencil or crayon, rather than using the brush to paint areas.

Reactions such as these are normal because the very young child has not yet achieved control over his muscles and muscular movement to any great degree. He still walks awkwardly, waddles when he runs, sometimes has difficulty finding his mouth with his spoon, and so forth. As he gains control of muscular movement, he grows physically, emotionally, and socially.

Gesell states that at some point around two years of age the child, given crayon or pencil, will put marks on a piece of paper.[6] Millard, among others, has termed this "scribbling."[7] Lowenfeld indicates that at this level of development there are four stages which he labels: 1) without differentiation, 2) controlled, 3) circular, and 4) named.[8] Gaitskell also emphasizes the importance of this level of development but places the results in three categories: 1) random manipulation, 2) controlled manipulation, and 3) named manipulation.[9]

The child learns control of muscles and movement through constant use and thus begins refinement of his scribbles and squeezes little by little. At first he puts marks on a paper because of pure kinesthetic pleasure. As time progresses, he will put more lines on more paper because he now likes to do it out of a sense of accomplishment. Regardless of the number of steps in this stage of development, there will come a time when the child will put a title to his drawing, his piece of clay work, or his construction. As an art teacher you must realize that this is a very subjective effort and that it is more than likely the meaning will escape you when the work is judged by adult standards. The

[6] Arnold Gesell, *How a Baby Grows* (New York: Harper & Brothers, 1945).

[7] Cecil V. Millard, *Childhood Growth and Development in the Elementary School Years* (Boston: D. C. Heath & Company, 1951), p. 110.

[8] Viktor Lowenfeld, *Creative and Mental Growth* (3d ed.; New York: The Macmillan Co., 1957), pp. 87-90.

[9] Charles D. Gaitskell, *Children and Their Art* (New York: Harcourt, Brace & Co., 1958), p. 129.

The manipulative stage begins about the age of two. This is the age of "scrib-bling." The child manipulates art materials to meet physical needs as well as to have an outlet for creative expression.

title might have been arrived at by the movement involved, the color, the asso-ciations, or by any number of other means.

Presymbolic Stage

While this stage of the developmental sequence of creative activity is largely based on the manipulative stage, it has certain earmarks which lend an importance to this level. Usually there is a relationship to reality and the "naming" of the parts by the child. Sections of a paper may be covered by a drawing while other sections are left blank. The concern of the child at this level of development is not with adult concepts of composition, but as de Francesco says, "the concern of the child is emotional and nonrealistic."[10] This is the stage when the child is self-centered. Psychologists tell us that this is the age of "mine," "me," "I," and "my." Art experiences will be centered around activities relating to the child.

Symbolic Stage

This is the true phase of symbols in the child's creative efforts. The control of materials and tools which the child gains by constant manipulation increases the concept of "man" and "things" around him. It is at this level that the efforts of the child begin to have meaning to the adult as well as the child. But while the individual child will develop well-defined representations, there is a wide variety of symbols used among children as a group and even within the creative development of one child. Goodenough[11] and later Gaitskell[12] find this to be true. Gaitskell further discovers that at this level of achievement sex enters the picture in that preference in subject matter is found.[13] At times symbols used by children in this stage are still quite subjective.

At this level the "X-ray" picture often comes into being. In this kind of picture, the so-called inside-outside relationships are exhibited.

Beginning Realism Stage

Usually during the 4th or 5th grade in school the child begins to shed the well-defined symbols of the past. At the same time drawings, especially, take on some of the qualities of realism—backgrounds, middle grounds, foregrounds, and perspective-like drawing. A more definite interest in color emerges in terms of color quality. Usually during the same period the child renews interest in flat design.

Drawing, construction, design, and color activities in which the child engages at this level are more natural than planned. The teacher does not conscientiously teach rules and regulations, but instead, provides the opportunity and facilities with which to work. De Francesco makes the statement that "formal teaching of any sort is not only futile but actually thwarting."[11]

10 Italo L. de Francesco, *Art Education, Its Means and Ends* (New York: Harper & Brothers, 1958), p. 254.

11 Florence E. Goodenough, "Children's Drawings," *A Handbook of Child Psychology* (Worcester: Clark University Press, 1931).

12 Gaitskell, *op. cit.*, pp. 131-133.

13 *Ibid.*, p. 135.

14 De Francesco, *op. cit.*, p. 264.

Stage of Reasoning

This is the level of development in which the child begins the analysis of life and environmental situations. Because of this, de Francesco calls this level the stage of "analytical realism." Lowenfeld refers to the same stage as the stage of "reasoning." To put it briefly the student is becoming a curious organism and is beginning to be interested in solutions to problems and perplexing questions in the 6th and 7th grades. At this stage the pupil is undergoing a psychological change from childhood to young manhood in his personal and emotional life. It is realistic to assume that the growth taking place and the adjustment being made affect the creative expression of the pupil. This stage represents the bridge to adolescence.

At this level some art educators and psychologists have classified pupils into the several creative type categories. Actually this identification relates itself to the manner in which the child perceives or sees. Some of these groupings are extensive, some rather meager. Herbert Read's classifications are stated as "organic, emphatic, rhythmical pattern, structural form, enumerative, haptic, decorative, and imaginative."[15] Barclay-Russell categorizes the types as architectural, classical, decorative, dramatic, emotional, haptic, impressionist, intellectual, lyrical, mystic, romantic, simple storytelling, and two-dimensional.[16] Both of these descriptions, as typical classifications in a more or less clinical sense, are lengthy and rather complete.

Lowenfeld shortens the statement of creative types to two classifications: the visual minded, or those who see; and the haptic, or those who feel.[17] The visual minded type is one who is objective, a person interested in the appearance of things. He senses impersonally as a disinterested spectator observes. The haptic individual is conversely one who is extremely subjective in that he is interested more in the personal sensations aroused by tactile impressions. It must be stated that seldom will one find a true haptic or visual type; the point to be made is one of degree of visualness or the degree of the haptic. One classification almost always includes some of the other.

De Francesco indicates that these two categories are sufficient for the classroom. It is his contention that these types in pure state indicate the extremes of perception and that other categories, i.e., Read's classifications, might be the in-between types.[18]

---

[15] Herbert Read, *Education Through Art* (New York: Pantheon Books, Inc., 1945), p. 141.

[16] A. Barclay-Russell, "Art and the Adolescent," *Education and Art, A Symposium* (Paris: UNESCO), pp. 46-49.

[17] Lowenfeld, *op. cit.*, pp. 262-277.

[18] De Francesco, *op. cit.*, p. 268.

Adolescent Stage

The previously mentioned developmental levels are almost exclusively in the province of the elementary school. When a child reaches the age of 12 or 13, he is in the early adolescent years and begins to approach manhood. Physically, psychologically, and socially there are many changes which take place. His life begins to take on some purpose, his ideas begin to take shape, and his social adjustment to adulthood begins.

In his creative efforts he begins to seek perfection in his endeavors. He becomes more interested in the end product rather than the process, the material, or the motive. The creative effort becomes enhanced by the vocational aspect as the student progresses through the high school art program. There are many such programs which have an actual vocational emphasis, with such well-defined and delimited courses of study as "Interior Design," "Commercial Art," "Jewelry Crafts," and so forth. During the high school ages, in many instances, the changing emphasis is from one of experimentation on a cafeteria-like basis to one of exploration in a narrower field.

Because of the special needs, abilities, and interests of the high school pupil, the art teacher needs to differentiate in planning, motivation, and teaching. Several authorities stress two ways of organizing an art program which bear investigation at least. Of course the individual situation, such as the size of the school, the type of the school population, the budget available, and so forth, all bear on these programs.

One of these programs is based on the "general art" approach. This approach assumes that all high school students will benefit from such a program in terms of a better understanding, deeper interests, and sounder standards of taste. Such a program can be developed in almost any situation but is particularly of interest in the smaller school.

The second program is that of the "art major" approach. In most instances there are several "courses" which can be chosen, normally by the talented few. Such a program indicates broader experiences and opportunities for the gifted and interested student rather than the narrow specialization found in some schools. Regardless of the point of departure in secondary school art program structure, the art teacher and the school administrator must remember the established goals of the program as mentioned in Chapter 2.

Summary

In this chapter the developmental stages of growth in terms of creative abilities have been noted. It was stated that the several authorities define these stages in a similar manner, although different names are applied to the several levels. In turn, a brief statement of six stages of creative growth was made.

These stages include the manipulative stage, the presymbolic stage, the symbolic stage, the beginning realism stage, the stage of reasoning, and the adolescent stage. A chart indicating the titling of these levels as determined by several authorities was included. An art teacher needs to know the measure and nature of creative development at the different age-grade levels, especially if he is to plan, teach, and evaluate the art program in the public schools.

For Further Reading

Barclay-Russell, A., "Art and the Adolescent," *Education and Art, A Symposium,* Paris: UNESCO.

Cole, Natalie R., *The Arts in the Classroom,* New York: The John Day Co., 1942.

De Francesco, Italo L., *Art Education, Its Means and Ends,* New York: Harper & Brothers, 1958.

Gaitskell, Charles D., *Children and Their Art,* New York: Harcourt, Brace & Co., 1958.

Gesell, Arnold, *How a Baby Grows,* New York: Harper & Brothers, 1945.

Goodenough, Florence E., "Children's Drawings," *A Handbook of Child Psychology,* Worcester: Clark University Press, 1931.

Lowenfeld, Viktor, *Creative and Mental Growth,* 3d ed.; New York: The Macmillan Co., 1957.

Mathias, Margaret, *Art in the Elementary School,* New York: Charles Scribner's Sons, 1929.

Mendelowitz, Daniel M., *Children Are Artists,* Stanford: Stanford University Press, 1953.

Millard, Cecil V., *Child Growth and Development in the Elementary School Years,* Boston: D. C. Heath & Company, 1951.

Read, Herbert, *Education Through Art,* New York: Pantheon Books, Inc., 1945.

Reed, Carl, *Early Adolescent Art Education,* Peoria: Charles A. Bennett Co., Inc., 1957.

For Further Thinking and Doing

1. Make a collection of children's drawings for each grade from kindergarten through grade six. Select three from each grade: low for the grade, average, and high for the grade in terms of creative growth. Determine the overlapping of abilities as contrasted with the age-grade placement of the pupil.
2. Make a collection of drawings showing each of the six stages of creative development as described in this chapter.
3. Test your ability to recognize the "haptic" and the "visual" types by making selections from children's drawings of the fifth and sixth grades.

Method and Good Teaching

METHODOLOGY in art teaching refers to the ways of presenting the learning situation to the children in a class—how to teach art. Such a topic is exceptionally broad in scope and cannot be treated fully in this work. You have probably had an introduction to methodology in your college classes prior to reading this book. For that reason only the high points will be touched on in this chapter. Other considerations of methodology will be alluded to in other chapters. Suffice it to say that teaching procedures in art are presented here as a review and not as original information.

Several Teaching Methods

Teaching methods in art can be grouped into several categories, but the present discussion will include only four general methods.

DIRECTED METHOD. Normally, different types of art activities and their several purposes would require different approaches and presentations. However, some teachers of art seemingly never vary their teaching method, nor, in fact, seem to have more than one. One of the most common methods, and perhaps the oldest, is that called the "directed" method.

Landis describes this teaching approach in art as "that practice which requires the child to follow certain prescribed rules and directions."[1] In this method of teaching, decisions regarding the end product, the technique of execution, and the media used are made by the teacher. Rules and regulations are imposed or dictated. In other words, the teacher decides for the children *what* is to be done, *why* it is to be done, and *how* it is to be done. As de Francesco indicates, this approach infers that "the student is in school to learn and the teacher is there to teach."[2] According to some teachers in the field, this

[1] Mildred Landis, *Meaningful Art Education* (Peoria: Chas. A. Bennett Co., Inc., 1951), p. 13.

[2] Italo L. de Francesco, *Art Education, Its Means and Ends* (New York: Harper & Brothers, 1958), p. 133.

approach is adopted with an eye to an "objective" result. However, in such a program because it is a teacher dominated situation, there is little opportunity on the part of the children for experimentation or originality—no subjectivity, that quality which makes most works of art great.

While it is easy to condemn this method of teaching on many grounds, there are instances where it can be used to advantage. The areas in which it can be used to some advantage are with older students and in situations where some sort of specific techniques must be mastered. It is conceivable that such a situation could arise in teaching some of the more mechanistic aspects of the art program where a step-by-step following of directions is necessary. Teaching the use of specific tools and equipment, formal perspective, mechanical drawing, and so forth are fair examples of common activities in which the "directed" method of teaching art and art techniques *could* be acceptable. But one must be cautioned in using this approach because it becomes stifling to creative learning in any field.

SELF-EXPRESSION. The so-called self-expression, or "free-expression," method as it is sometimes termed, is the antithesis of the "directed" method. In the "directed" method everything depends on the teacher. In the "self-expression" approach little, if anything, depends on the teacher. In such a procedure the end product, technique, accomplishment, and often the media to be used are decided upon by the student, usually without guidance. The art experience is student-dominated. This approach allows for a maximum of freedom for the student because the student decides for himself *what* he wants to do and *how* he wants to do it. Usually there is little reason behind the choice except that the child "likes" to do this.

"Self-expression" as a teaching approach keeps the child "happy" and "cheerful." By having this as a major goal, one wonders what the child is actually accomplishing. Since this method usually involves minimum teacher activity or action, the child can approach his desired activity with improper attitudes and incorrect procedures. He is doing nothing more than making bigger and better mistakes. There are those who say that giving a child an opportunity to do and make such decisions for himself is wholesome for the child. It is also said that, in certain cases, castor oil is good for a child, although, the author cannot remember enjoying even the prospect of being submitted to the cure.

This method lacks purpose—if one can justify what happens as method. Since there are no limits within which to work and no established goals for the activity, pupils who are originally thankful for such a situation in the classroom soon become listless and disinterested in their efforts and in their results. Such will be the effect with continuous usage. The pupil is not being challenged when he makes all the decisions himself. "No competent and responsible educational leader ever said anywhere at any time that the pupil is to do what he wants to do."[3] Again, as in the case of the "directed" method of teaching art, there can be some sort of justification attempted on occasion for employing this method.

When such a teaching procedure is used continually, one would suspect that the teacher is either mentally or professionally lazy or is professionally incompetent. It takes little education for a teacher to come into a classroom and say: "draw something." However, when and if a student should finish an assigned task, is it not then in good order to have him decide what he might like to do on his own concerning art experiences, materials, and the styles he would like to use? One should constantly keep in mind one word mentioned before— "guidance." This is one of the basic duties of the teacher, to guide youth. A teacher cannot guide a pupil in his work if the pupil is doing the work on his own while the teacher is correcting papers, working on the attendance record, or filling out insurance receipts. It is suggested that few teachers have the gift to use the "self-expression" method wisely and that, therefore, it is to be used only after much planning, or avoided altogether as far as the beginning teacher is concerned.

INTEGRATION. Integration is as much concerned with curriculum building as it is with method. While it is a manner of teaching, this approach depends to a large extent, on the construction of the curriculum. Winslow says that "the curriculum cannot afford to be anything short of life itself in which all areas contribute to effective living."[4] Or, as de Francesco says, "The meaning of integration in the teaching of art involves the totality of the creative experience."[5]

It is possible that Landis has this teaching method in mind when she describes what she calls "meaningful art education," the relationship of means to ends in art education.[6]

In integrative teaching many areas of learning are combined into a united whole to give meaning to a particular activity. The visible creative solution to a problem under discussion will depend on the age group with which you are dealing, their desires in experimentation, and the materials available.

"If art education is to function fully in the lives of boys and girls, art must be made to permeate most of the activities that they engage in . . . ."[7]

---

[3] William H. Burton, *The Guidance of Learning Activities* (2d ed.; New York: Appleton-Century-Crofts, Inc., 1952), p. 65.

[4] Leon L. Winslow, *The Integrated School Art Program* (New York: McGraw-Hill Book Co., 1949), p. 37.

[5] De Francesco, *op. cit.,* p. 147.

[6] Landis, *op. cit.,* p. 22.

[7] Winslow, *op. cit.,* p. 33.

Integrated teaching involves learning which is related to many areas. The art aspect of an integrated experience having to do with Pennsylvania history is illustrated here. Students are constructing historical models to be placed on a relief map of the state.

In actual practice integrative teaching in art involves learning in many related areas; it involves selection, analysis, examination, and evaluation of the total problem, and, therefore, of the total result.

A six-week unit of work was decided on by a sixth grade class in Connellsville, Pennsylvania, several years ago in an experimentation with integrative teaching.[8] The general title of the unit of work was "Pennsylvania," one of the topics in the state-suggested course of study for the sixth grade in social studies. At the end of the six-week period the visible creative effort was a relief map of the state and models of historic spots of significance. Before all this could happen, the pupils learned something of geography, history, important scientific discoveries, and exploration. The mathematics of fractions were taught in order to learn the use of the ruler for measurements and scale; further interests were literary figures and their work, the importance of music, vocabulary, and experi-

[8] Sherrick Fisher, "Connellsville School Tries Unit Approach," *Pennsylvania School Journal,* XCVIII, No. 8 (April, 1950), pp. 310-311.

ence to improve ability to write. When all this was assimilated by the class, they were ready to put to work some of the principles and facts they had learned and to crystallize their experience into concrete form.

A junior art class in a high school in Illinois became interested in the artistic contributions to the theatre.[9] While the final result was a model stage for experimentation with scene design, pupils had to progress through many activities and learnings before the final form was reached:

1. Mechanical drawing—the use of instruments and techniques for drawing the plans.
2. Woodworking—construction involving the use of hand tools and a knowledge of finishes of wood.
3. Sewing—the use of materials for drapes and curtains and their construction.
4. Electricity—wiring and construction of footlights and borders, together with a panel box.
5. Art—set design of cardboard and paint made to scale for planned productions of the drama department.

The result of all this learning and activity was a model stage with a complete lighting system that could be used experimentally for set designs year after year.

In the examples cited, the art teacher was the important focal point. Other teachers were brought into the activity to give technical information and guidance. But the art teacher met the criteria stated by de Francesco when he says that in this type of teaching "a good teacher can provide through art education, a varied array of experiences. . . . This variety has been advocated for a long time as a basic condition of a well-balanced curriculum."[10]

Integrative teaching is a more difficult method to pursue because exceptionally broad planning must take place as well as detailed planning for technical aspects of the activities involved. But if the end result of the learnings which take place are important to the child as part of the education of a whole person, the method and the time spent are well used.

CORRELATION. Correlation has been termed by some leaders in the field of teaching as "parallel teaching."

In essence a correlated approach to teaching in art is the use of subject matter from another area of knowledge as the springboard for the creative activity. In practice this means that the art teacher knows, or finds out, what is being studied in history, geography, and other subject areas. The art teacher then plans his work as complement to the other area or, as the current phrase describes it, as an enrichment experience.

[9] Wellington B. Gray, "Integration, It's Easy," *Illinois Education*, XL, No. 9 (May, 1952), p. 354.
[10] De Francesco, *op. cit.*, p. 149.

There are several objections to this method of teaching art. Among them the criticism that art becomes a "servant" to other fields, and that this method builds artificial barriers and relationships.

While this teaching method takes a good amount of planning, an art teacher who really knows his business can make the creative experience as important as the area of learning with which art is being correlated. He can also indicate to his students with ease the correct relationships which exist between art and the correlated area.

Aspects of Teaching Methods

Although we could expand on basic methodology there are some aspects of approaches to teaching art specifically which need to be defined in rather precise terms. Two of these aspects are motivation and helping the student.

Motivation. It has been stated that motivation is the most important part of teaching as far as the teacher *or* the student is concerned. Without some kind of motivation there would be a poor attitude at best and resultant slip-shod work. With proper motivation, the entire picture changes. Basically, motivation can be divided into four main parts, each important in itself but each, to some extent, dependent on the others. These four parts are what may be called: the "build-up," the "sample," giving suggestions, and questions and answers.

The Build-Up—Gaining the interest of the student and getting him excited about the problem at hand is a big job. This is especially true with pupils in the junior and senior high school art courses, and even more so if they are there because they can't fit into the academic program of the secondary school. Of course this may be poor administration and guidance work, but criticism of these areas is not the purpose of the present work. Almost everyone who teaches art has the difficult task of interesting pupils in the art work. However, most teachers follow a similar pattern in the motivation technique with success.

It is usual to lead into the problem itself in a general and gradual manner and to do this slowly. The teacher should not present himself to the class and make a definite statement, arbitrarily, such as: "Today we are going to make etched copper bracelets." Rather, he leads into the problem under consideration or contemplation gradually, so that pupils become more and more interested and begin to want to try the proposed activity. The teacher should now ask questions which are at least stimulating, questions which get the pupil to think. Some background of the article, technique, or process could and probably should be introduced at an early time. Some of the uses of the article, technique, or process contemplated should be mentioned to indicate the importance of the activity in everyday life.

The important thing to remember is that the job of the art teacher is to build up the enthusiasm of the student to the point where he really wants to do the work about to be presented and to do it well. At times modifications in the plan might have to be made due to an exceptional amount of enthusiasm in a particular phase of the project. Should this occur, the adjustment should be made if at all possible.

The older the pupil is with whom the teacher is dealing, the more time he must put into the motivation process. Usually younger pupils in the elementary school take to new ideas, techniques, and materials quite readily. In fact, there are times when it is all the teacher can do to hold back these pupils from pushing ahead before the are really ready. Many times just the mention of the problem which has bee planned is enough to get boys and girls started in earnest.

Whatever the motivation technique used to gain and hold the interest, plan the attack with as much detail as possible. This kind of planning makes for a better attitude and for a better quality of work.

The Sample—"Sample" is another way to say example. It is always wise to use an example of the completed problem for display and interest. As has been mentioned, smaller children tend to seek the approval of the teacher. If the child thinks that the "sample" is the kind of thing that should result from his efforts, his work will more often than not look like the example displayed. For this reason it is wise to use several different samples. Don't keep them up before boys and girls during all the time the activity is being presented or when the children are working. A better way to show the "sample" is to display it while you are talking about specifics of the problem, and then put the "sample" away.

Students in high school will not tend to copy what is displayed. They like to have the "sample" around to check from time to time as to size, appropriate details, and so forth. They also like to have it around to make sure that theirs is at least different and is a definite improvement over the "sample." The teacher's own experience will indicate the best way to use the "sample" as children differ from grade to grade, school to school, and city to city. A word of caution: Use pupil work if at all possible so that pupils can see what someone of their own age group can and has done in the past. If you use professional or your own work, very likely the pupils will strive for slick perfection rather than originality of thought.

Guidance—Giving guidance to the class is also part of the technique of motivation. There are two schools of thought on giving guidance to the class. The first is that technical directions should be step-by-step, as detailed as possible for all parts of the procedure. Experience has shown that when this is the case, most of the resulting work will look like so many carbon copies. There are times, in very intricate techniques and processes, when a certain amount of this is necessary. However, this teaching device should be used sparingly so that originality and creativity are the important results.

The second school of thought on giving guidance to pupils maintains that sufficient direction to insure successful completion of the problem is all that is necessary. It is maintained that, if complete directions are given in all phases of the project, there will be little opportunity for the pupil to think or to function as an individual. It is the contention that a broad outline of the art experience and/or process involved should be given, within which the student can plot his own course to satisfy his own needs.

Except in highly technical cases the second philosophy seems to have considerably more on its side of the argument than does the first. The more directions given, the more rules and regulations imposed, the more sterile the resultant art product becomes.

Questions and Answers—As part of the motivation process the art teacher should always allow time for questions from the class before each student begins his own work. In this manner you can once again hit at the business of taking care of individual differences and needs in the class. If one particular student seems to have a very great problem, speak with him individually so that you will not waste the time of the entire class.

When answering questions, give a concise, clear answer as quickly as possible. Give a positive answer; don't hedge. Above all, don't be afraid to admit you are wrong or have made a mistake—all of us are human. But don't make mistakes any more than you can help. Give an honest answer; don't be a "phony." The pupils will catch on very soon if you continually put them off or give a light comment to a serious question. Be serious when answering questions; they are usually asked in all seriousness by students.

"HELPING" THE STUDENT. There are many ways of helping the student. Some of them are more of a hindrance than a help, depending on the manner in which the helping is done. Three kinds of helps, among many, are the demonstration, working on the student's material, and giving advice. Each of these forms of help is important to successful completion of the problem in many cases; each should be planned as much as possible (especially the demonstration); and each is part of the teaching technique.

Demonstration—Whenever possible the teacher should demonstrate new or unfamiliar techniques and materials to those students who are in need of the information. The demonstration needs to be timed properly; it must be performed when it can be of greatest benefit to the students involved. This is to say that a demonstration of the complete processes necessary for the ultimate

Demonstrations by the student teacher or by an expert are
intended to exemplify a process. Pupils will then bend their ener-
gies to creating their own work with a knowledge of mechanics.

creation is not advisable when the problem is introduced. As the time approaches when a particular process is necessary information, then is the time to perform the demonstration.

Several rules apropos of the demonstration are:

1. Be sure that you have all necessary equipment, materials, and supplies available for the demonstration. Be sure that the equipment and supplies used in the demonstration will be the same as those the pupils are to use. Have the equipment and material arranged in logical order so that you, the teacher, will not have to hunt through a confused pile to find what you need.

2. As you use each piece of equipment and each bit of material, give its correct name and explain its use. Do not refer to specific equipment as "this gadget," and so forth. Use correct terminology.

3. Go through the demonstration step by step, explaining materials, tools, and processes in plain language and as directly as possible. There is no purpose nor anything to be gained by presenting a master's thesis to a junior high school art class.

4. Group the students around the work bench or table at which the demonstration is to be performed, in comfort, and so that each member of the class can see and hear well.

5. Allow time for questions which pupils undoubtedly will have. Handle questions as they arise during the demonstration rather than all at the end. This will avoid misunderstandings when it is important to clear them up. Of course, allow time also at the end of the demonstrations so that any loose ends may be picked up by answering questions.

6. Be clear, concise, and correct. The visual act of demonstration is retained much longer than the words which would be necessary were there no demonstration. Should you make an error in procedure, correct it immediately and admit that the error was made.

Working on the Student's Creative Effort—"Helping" a pupil by demonstrating on his own work poses several problems. The amount of good or harm done depends on whether the teacher helps directly on the pupil's project and the extent of this type of help.

There are teachers who paint, draw, and so forth on a pupil's work in order to demonstrate something specific in the way of color, technique, and the like, having a direct relationship only to the *particular* student's problem. The pupil will have a particular question at a specific point in the process and needs help at that time. Consequently, the teacher works on the pupil's efforts in order to save time. The pupil does not have the time to wait until a similar point is reached on a demonstration piece of work, especially done for his benefit by the teacher, similar to his. This procedure is fraught with dangers and should seldom be used.

A better way of helping the pupil is to draw or paint on a piece of material belonging to the teacher. Many art teachers make it a practice to have a pad of "scratch" paper available on which they can demonstrate by making a quick sketch. As he makes the rounds of the class, he uses this pad to illustrate points he wishes to make for the help of individual pupils.

A teacher in a very large Midwest high school found that the enrollment in her art classes was rapidly decreasing because she was helping the pupils too much on their own work. In a typical project having to do with posters, the teacher required that each student present work to her before handing it in for a final grade. As each student brought his work to the teacher's drafting table, he would find that the teacher thought "this ought to be fixed up a bit" and "something else ought to be done" here and there. The teacher would then delve into the pile of material on her desk and start to paint on the poster. Finally, when the last poster was submitted for inspection, all the posters had a sameness about them because the teacher had worked on each of them and had given her own peculiar sign of craftsmanship to each.

What we have in such a situation is the work of the teacher and the student and not the creation of the student alone. How would the teacher evaluate such a piece of "creativity" as described above? Or could he evaluate it at all?

Giving Advice—One of the most helpful things teachers can do is to move about the class from pupil to pupil giving advice and encouragement as to how the pupil's drawing or construction can be improved. Give praise when a good job is in process. By understanding how the creation can be improved, the pupil is learning as an individual, the resulting art activity is more pleasing to the eye, and the pupil will learn how to take criticism in the proper manner.

Giving advice to pupils as described in Chapter 8, "Aspects of Evaluation," is also an important way in which to help the student. This type of criticism comes after the problem has been completed and takes into account comments by other pupils as well as the teacher.

All criticism should be direct and honest. Finding fault for the sake of having something to say is not good teaching. Judgments can be positive as well as negative. If the pupil is doing or has done a commendable piece of work, tell him about it. This sort of commendation keeps the pupil learning, interested, and productive.

Summary

In this chapter we have given some consideration to teaching methods in art. Those referred to have been termed the directed method, self-expression, integrative teaching, and correlation. While these are not all the mehods which could be listed, they are the most common in use.

In addition to the approaches stated, we have considered some aspects of art teaching methods. Under the heading of motivation we mentioned the "build-up," and "sample," giving guidance, and questions and answers. In discussing how to help the pupils in their work, we considered the demonstration, working on the pupil's project, and giving critical help.

There is no one method of teaching art. The specific task and the child involved in the creative experience will often dictate the approach to the teaching act. A poor teacher can wreck the best method; a good teacher can adapt almost any method successfully. Only after the child has been motivated to achieve the limits of his capabilities can a teaching method be termed a success.

Whatever the approach used in teaching art, the student teacher should relate the method used to his philosophy of art education. There must be a direct relationship between the approach to teaching and the end purposes or goals one wishes to achieve by teaching. In Chapter 2 we discussed the philosophy of art education as to aesthetic development, expression through art education, good citizenship, and the creative potential of the child. If these four elements are necessary purposes to a successful art program, the teacher must ask the question: What method or methods will allow me to achieve these goals for the boys and girls whom I teach?

For Further Reading

Burton, William H., *The Guidance of Learning Activities,* 2d ed.; New York: Appleton-Century-Crofts, Inc., 1952.

Cronbach, Lee J., *Educational Psychology,* New York: Harcourt, Brace & Co., 1954.

De Francesco, Italo L., *Art Education, Its Means and Ends,* New York: Harper & Brothers, 1958.

Dewey, John, *Experience and Education,* New York: The Macmillan Co., 1938.

Fisher, Sherrick, "Connellsville School Tries Unit Approach," *Pennsylvania School Journal,* XCVIII, No. 8 (April, 1950).

Gray, Wellington B., "Integration, It's Easy," *Illinois Education,* XL, No. 9 (May, 1952).

Jersild, Arthur T., *Child Psychology,* Englewood Cliffs: Prentice-Hall, Inc., 1954.

Landis, Mildred M., *Meaningful Art Education,* Peoria: Chas. A. Bennett Co., Inc., 1951.

McDonald, Rosabel, *Art as Education,* New York: Henry Holt & Co., Inc., 1941.

Mort, Paul R. and Vincent, William S., *Modern Educational Practice,* New
     York: McGraw-Hill Book Co., 1950.
Schultz, Harold and Shores, Harlan, *Art in the Elementary Schools,* Urbana:
     University of Illinois Press, 1948.
Winslow, Leon L., *The Integrated School Art Program,* New York: McGraw-
     Hill Book Co., 1949.

For Further Thinking and Doing

1. Observe a master art teacher present several lessons to children. List the
   motivational devices used by this teacher.
2. During your observations, keep a running tally on the several methods used
   by art teachers. Which methods seem to be more popular? Is there any
   obvious correlation between the age, preparation, and experience of the
   teacher and the teaching method used?
3. To what extent and in what way does the master art teacher "help" the
   student in his work?

5

Planning For Teaching

THE teaching process is long and involved. One just does not get up before a class and start lecturing or painting. A relatively small percentage of the time is actually spent before the class in the act of teaching. Most of the time is spent in the planning stages, prior to appearing in the classroom or studio.

It is not our purpose in this chapter to discuss the entire art program of the public schools. It is our purpose to discuss the individual teaching operation, although you should know that in practice one must become part of the other.

Lesson Plan

As has been stated in several instances, most teaching takes a vast amount of planning. One must know what is to be taught in order to do justice to the pupil, the subject, the materials, and the time involved. Then one must determine how it is to be taught. For this one must plan, and PLAN, and *PLAN*. In order to help young teachers in their work, the following material is presented as a guide for teaching organization in the art program. Each of the following major headings would be a separate division in a "lesson plan." However, these may not be all the topics which would be necessary or which one might wish to include for use. It must also be added that this type of organization is not original with the author, but that it is quite a common thing in many institutions where art education is an important part of the total program. An example of such a lesson plan is to be found on page 42.

STATEMENT OF THE ART EXPERIENCE. At the beginning of the lesson plan, it is wise to have a simple, direct statement of what is to be accomplished in the lesson. Make the statement positive; a simple phrase such as "to produce a mobile using foil paper and coat hangers" is sufficient. The whole purpose of this section of the lesson plan is to indicate what is to happen during the art period.

AIMS. An "Aim" is a long-range goal. In this section the teacher should list the part or parts this particular art activity plays in the long-range art educa-

EAST CAROLINA COLLEGE
Greenville, North Carolina

LESSON PLAN

I. STATEMENT OF PROBLEM

II. AIMS (Long Range Goals)

III. OBJECTIVES (Short Range Goals)

IV. MATERIALS

V. PROCEDURES

VI. EVALUATION

VII. OUTCOMES

VIII. SOURCES AND RESOURCES

tion of the student. As an example, clay modeling in the elementary school program will develop muscular coordination and the muscles themselves. Thus, an aim in clay modeling could be to build muscles and to develop muscular control. Muscular control cannot be achieved entirely in one art period—it takes years of doing, and thus it is a long-range goal—an aim.

OBJECTIVES. An "Objective" is an immediate goal. It differs from an aim in that one can hope to achieve the objective within the time span alloted to one art experience. As an illustration, in a problem dealing with lettering, an objective could be to teach the use of the lettering pen. While the pupil will perhaps not become proficient or perfect in using the lettering pen, he will at least have a formal introduction to the lettering pen and know what to do and how to do it. Under the heading of the objectives for a lesson plan one should list those major accomplishments which can be achieved during the lesson.

MATERIALS. It is imperative that the student teacher know just what equipment and materials of instruction are necessary for the accomplishment of the activity at hand. Regardless of how trifling the material or equipment might be, without it the project might not be finished. Therefore, everything necessary from the lowly thumb tack to the electric kiln, from the pencil to the acid bath should be listed. In this way the teacher has a complete list of the things that are necessary.

PROCEDURE. The procedure is what the teacher actually does in the teaching act and what the pupil must do in order to complete the art problem successfully. The procedure includes two parts, the first of which is the teacher's.

The first thing the teacher must do is to motivate the class. By this we mean that the teacher must interest the individual pupil in the art activity. The teacher must make the pupil want to do the proposed art work. In order to do this, the teacher should explain why the activity is important, what can be learned by having the experience, and must show the pupil some of the possibilities by exhibiting examples of completed projects similar to what the pupil could do. The teacher must understand that there is a direct relationship between the quality of motivation and the quality of interest and the resultant work. Therefore, the teacher should do the best possible job of motivation in order to get the best possible job and the most original bit of work out of the pupil. For a more detailed discussion of motivation turn to Chapter 4.

The second part of the procedure has to do with the specific directions on how to accomplish the task at hand. There are many considerations which must be recognized under the heading of procedures. The pupil must plan; that is, he must get ideas down on paper, make sketches, gather material, and so forth. Then he must make a good drawing or transfer the sketch to craft material.

Following this, the pupil must go through a step by step development to complete the project. Some activities are quite complicated because of the many different processes involved. Others are repetitious, in which one process is repeated over and over, as in weaving.

When the basic activity is completed, the pupil must "finish" it. He must polish, lacquer, press, mat, or frame it, depending of course on the kind of art experience and the materials used. There are times when finishing becomes part of the total procedure, as in the framing of a painting which has been completed.

6 —   EVALUATION. An evaluation is actually a critique of a completed problem from two standpoints. The first is an evaluation for the pupil. Ultimately this means that the pupil is assigned a grade for his completed work. However, there is usually more to an evaluation for the pupil than the assignment of a grade. It has been found that a class discussion with students offering positive as well as negative comments is a good way to hold a critique. Teachers are often surprised at the genuine frankness with which pupils discuss one another's work, without snide remarks or without hurting feelings. In such a discussion the teacher provides leadership in getting pupils to evaluate the art activity and to make suggestions for improvements in the future.

Secondly, the teacher must evaluate the art experience for himself in terms of its relative importance as a teaching technique and a learning device. The teacher must decide in what ways the activity was a success, where it fell down, and how it could be improved for future use. A supervisor of art in the South recently had a problem involving plaster for her teachers to work with. Because of climatic conditions at the particular time, the plaster dried too fast to be of much use. In the critique of the problem, the supervisor explained the effect of temperature and humidity on materials such as plaster and suggested that teachers should not use it again under similar conditions. For obvious reasons the section of the lesson plan on evaluation is usually left blank until after the project has been completed.

7 -   OUTCOMES. Beyond the art object, the teacher must determine what learnings and techniques were acquired and what materials were explored as a result of the creative efforts of pupils. This must not be confused with the listing of "Aims" and "Objectives" at the beginning of the lesson plan. They can be, but are not necessarily the same. There are times when art work takes a decided turn away from its original planned course. A teacher will make such an adjustment if the adjustment is likely to result in a better learning situation for the pupil. This is good teaching. In such circumstances, the outcomes could be decidedly different from the aims and objectives listed.

A teacher and his pupils in the Midwest planned to make murals as an enlargement of a painting problem. Pupils began to enlarge on the mural idea to the point where they received the school administration's approval to paint murals on the walls of the cafeteria. The murals were to depict the story of food: growing, processing, shipping, preparing and serving the various dishes in the cafeteria. The result, however, was a long way from the planned 4 x 8 foot murals for which they had made plans.

As is true with all evaluation, one must wait until the art activity has been finished before this part of the plan can be completed.

SOURCES AND RESOURCES. Under this heading the teacher should list all possible sources of materials—reference and visual materials—which will help solve the art problem in any way. Lists of books, articles, movies, slides, film strips, photos, records, and so forth should be as complete as possible. The reason for such a listing is to have all the information relative to the art project in one place, without having to search through pages and pages of material.

Unit Plan

There is only one basic difference between a lesson plan and a unit plan. A lesson plan is the teaching outline for a simple problem that involves but one process and can be completed by the pupil in a matter of one or two days. An example would be an illustration of an event by third graders. A unit plan involves the teaching of a "unit" of work which usually involves several processes and which could take a considerably longer time period than a lesson does. Actually, several lesson plans are used in the construction of a unit plan because related information, research, experimentation, and several processes are usually involved. The construction of a piece of jewelry with the possible processes of cutting the stone, polishing the stone, construction of the mounting, setting the stone, polishing the setting, and so forth is a good example of a unit plan because many different processes and activities and the use of different tools, techniques, and materials are involved in a time-consuming experience.

Planning the Art Experience

It has been mentioned that there are basically two types of problems in art from a planning viewpoint: teacher-planned activities and teacher-pupil planned experiences. Both are important to a well-rounded art program.

TEACHER-PLANNED ACTIVITIES. Teacher-planned activities are often necessary. It is the responsibility of the art teacher to teach technical aspects of the art program and to establish continuity in the work throughout the year. It is necessary to plan the work logically so that the problems develop sequentially and with a view to balance of activities. It would be difficult to let pupils paint in oils, for instance, before they learned something of composition. It would like-

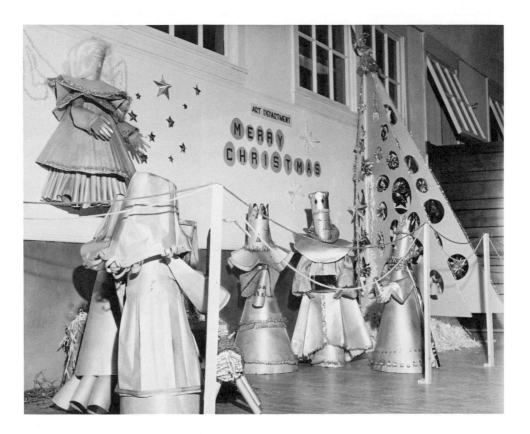

Group planning for learning experiences produces a democratic environment within which to work. Correlation of art with the holiday seasons, as above, gives a contemporary atmosphere in which holiday motivation makes for exciting creative expression.

wise be inadvisable for pupils to work in only one phase of art, i.e. jewelry making, for a whole year, especially if the student is not three-dimensionally minded. Therefore, one should expect the art teacher to plan within the framework of the syllabus or art guide in order to cover the work expected by the art supervisor.

TEACHER-PUPIL PLANNED EXPERIENCES. A well-developed program of art activities, and perhaps one which will yield best results in the long run, is a cooperative venture in which teachers and pupils share. The teacher's knowledge of the needs of her pupils, their inclinations, and their abilities will permit her to lead pupils in the selection of activities and processes most beneficial to their development. At the same time, pupils will feel responsible in that they have had a good share in making choices and in overall planning.

Pupil-planned experiences should enter the picture regularly to satisfy the individual needs and interests of the pupils and to practice classroom democracy. We often find that children who can draw well might not be able to work in three dimensions, such as crafts. The reverse is likewise true. It is important to the child to have him plan or help plan art activities at which he has a reasonable chance for success. After all, knowledge of design, color, etc. can be secured by working in the crafts just as well as by painting every day in the week. The teacher should remember, however, that the guidance is an indispensable part of the whole operation. In pupil-planned situations the children get a chance to develop plans for themselves and to do the job from start to finish. In this way they learn to rely on their own individual abilities and to practice democracy in the classroom by not having the particular art activity dictated.

Exhibitions and Publicity

To summarize the teaching process, it is advisable to display the work done by students in art classes in some manner. The music department exhibits its wares by having the band play at football games and in parades, and by having other musical organizations perform at concerts. Art teachers must call to the attention of the public what pupils in the art program are doing. One of the best ways to do this is by arranging exhibitions.

Quite often there are display facilities in the individual grade rooms of the elementary school. Bulletin boards and borders above the blackboards are the most general sources of space for the display of art work. This space can be utilized and the materials on exhibition can be changed as often as desirable.

Perhaps there is space in the halls where bulletin boards or display cases can be arranged. Committees of pupils could take care of running displays of art work each week or so, changing the exhibit when there is new and interesting material available for display.

Store windows in town and public places, such as the town library and other buildings, are usually available for the schools to use to display art work on occasion. It is well to keep this kind of facility for the more special exhibits during the school year. Each year in Connellsville, Pennsylvania, the merchants have turned over their store windows to the public school art teachers for display during Halloween, American Education Week, or National Art Week. In Highland Park, Illinois, a local building and loan company lent their display windows to the high school art director for an exhibition of scale-model homes designed and built by juniors in the high school. The local Sherwin-Williams

Well-planned exhibitions and publicity create good public relations and encourage pupils. Student teachers need to learn these techniques.

retail store in Greenville, North Carolina, regularly requests the college art department to provide exhibits for its display windows.

Many communities turn over all sorts of display facilities during special occasions such as American Education Week. This is the time when many parents are invited to visit the schools and special programs are presented in theaters and on radio and television. What an opportunity to exhibit the art work of the schools, to get their work before the general public and the parents in particular!

One must be cautioned about over-exhibiting. When this is done, teachers are forcing pupils to produce work so that exhibitions may be held. Out the window go all the purposeful aims and objectives of the program and teachers are compromising their philosophy in order to gain glory for the art program.

A further caution, especially concerning the elementary school child, is that teachers should make sure that at some time during the school year each and every pupil has something in an exhibition. Whether the work lacks perfection, whether the work is good, bad, or indifferent, matters little. What is important is that it be representative of the pupil's ability to produce in his own creative way. Some pupils will never achieve slick-looking work; nor, perhaps, should they attempt to.

The exhibition as a device for summarizing what has been attempted in the art program, more or less interprets for other students and the general public so that they can understand the importance of the art program to the individual pupil as well as to the entire community. The exhibition affords the layman opportunity to understand and evaluate the art program. It clarifies the function of creative and mental activities in total education, and it relates art to the community. The exhibition also aids in teaching by means of motivation, communication, and evaluation.[1]

Last but not least, have a reporter from the school paper pay you a visit regularly so that you can get the information about exhibitions before the school population. See that photographs (even if you have to take them yourself) and articles get into the local papers whether they are daily or weekly journals when there is something of interest to the entire community to be presented. Be sure that the school and community know that the program in art education is functioning, by periodic reminders in the press. All this is for the benefit of the pupils, the school, and the community.

Summary

In this chapter we have seen the numerous tasks with which the art teacher is faced in planning and carrying out the teaching act. The teacher must plan, motivate, discuss, demonstrate, answer questions, evaluate, prepare sources of information, exhibit, and publicize. Each of these parts of the planning process has peculiar techniques which can be used. Several suggestions have been made in this chapter for handling these problems. The art teacher will find that each school is different from every other school and that what works well in one will not necessarily work well in another. The teacher must plan his techniques so that they will fit the situation in which he finds himself. The suggestions given in this chapter are made only as guides, as one approach, and not as a cure-all and solution to all the art teacher's problems in planning.

[1] The Kutztown Bulletin, "The Exhibition," *Art Education at Work* (Kutztown: State Teachers College, 1953), pp. 3-4.

For Further Reading

Kainz, Louise C. and Riley, Olive L., *Exploring Art,* New York: Harcourt, Brace & Co., 1951.

The Kutztown Bulletin, "The Exhibition," *Art Education at Work,* Kutztown: State Teachers College, 1953.

Miel, Alice, and others, *Cooperative Procedures in Learning,* New York: Teachers College, Bureau of Publications, Columbia University, 1952.

Rannells, Edward W., *Art Education in the Junior High School,* Lexington: University of Kentucky Press, 1946.

Richardson, Marion, *Art and the Child,* Peoria: Chas. A. Bennett Co., Inc., 1952.

Schultz, Harold and Shores, Harlan, *Art in the Elementary Schools,* Urbana: University of Illinois Press, 1948.

For Further Thinking and Doing

1. Observe a master art teacher to determine how goals are established and who establishes them.
2. Have a conference with several master art teachers to determine the amount and kind of planning involved in presenting an art experience.
3. On what bases do pupils enter into the planning of the experiences in the art class? The social studies class? The science class?

6

Classroom Management

CLASSROOM management is nothing more than the organization of physical facilities and routines for the effective use of school time. Management includes conditions of temperature, ventilation, lighting, neatness, seating arrangements for pupils, attendance checking, control of pupil movement, and the arrangement of the physical equipment.

Temperature and Ventilation

The classroom temperature at times is controlled for the teacher by the heating plant. In older buildings the thermostat is usually located in the boiler-room and is controlled by the school engineer or the chief custodian. In more modern buildings each classroom has its own thermostat so that the temperature can be regulated individually for each classroom according to the activity taking place in the room, the number of children in the room, and the location of the room in relation to the "warm side" of the building.

If there are radiators in the classroom, they can usually be controlled by turning them off or on. If the heating plant is one of the type called forced air, the ventilators in each of the classrooms can be regulated so that more or less heat enters the room. But why is the heat a concern of the teacher?

This question can be answered simply if one realizes that, if the pupils are not physically comfortable, they will be distracted by being too cool or too warm. This will mean that they will become preoccupied with getting warmer or will become sleepy and listless by being too warm. The correct average temperature should be between 68 and 72 degrees Fahrenheit. It is an important part of the teacher's job to see that this temperature is maintained, if at all possible, for the best possible learning situation.

Ventilation is also important for the same reasons. If "climate conditioning" is installed in the school, the air flow can be regulated for ventilation. However, few schools have this kind of equipment, and one must rely on the amount of air that can be admitted by way of the windows. It is important to see that there are no drafts so that children will not catch cold. To do this the opening of windows and doors should be checked regularly. Window boards or glasses should be used in cool weather, or the windows should be opened from the top to help prevent drafts.

Illumination

Direct sunlight shining on the pupil's work or table tends to dazzle him and can result in eye strain which leads to headache, irritability, scowling, and so forth. Adjust natural light by lowering the window shades or by adjusting the blinds.

Shadows can be controlled to some degree by moving the pupil or by adjusting artificial lighting as well as natural lighting. Some of the lights in the ceiling can be turned on or off as the situation indicates. Pupils often sit in their own light, causing shadows with the results mentioned above. As far as artificial lighting is concerned, probably the most popular lighting for art rooms and laboratories is fluorescent lighting, a diffused kind of artificial lighting making no strong, direct shadows.

Recently, authorities have demonstrated that the use of green blackboards and yellow chalk are best for visibility when board use is important. Adequate natural or artificial lighting on the board is important to visibility as well as to eliminate reflections and glare.

Neatness

There is no excuse for not having a clean, neat, and attractive place for teaching and learning. The "anchor man" in the chain of cleanliness is the school custodian. Since he has the main responsibility for keeping the school clean, the teacher, who can make his task less tedious, needs to cooperate.

At the conclusion of each class period, be sure that the room is neat and clean for the next class. Pupils should be schooled early in the "clean-up detail." As dirt is accumulated, it should be cleaned up. If each pupil takes care of his own debris—papers on the floor, dried clay and paste on the desk top—there will be little else that needs doing except to put away the materials used.

Monitors can take care of putting away materials, such as scissors, rulers, paints, brushes, waterpans, and so forth. Others can pass the wastebasket. Still others can be responsible for rearranging the furniture if necessary. The class can be divided into groups, each group being responsible for the cleanup for a week. Or if the class is organized by stations, tables, or rows, this would be a natural division for such an activity.

The reference books and the periodical shelf—the classroom library— must be kept neat and presentable at all times, for neatness sake as well as for the sake of finding items conveniently. One pupil in each class can be designated as "librarian." When the class period comes to an end, books and magazines should be returned to their proper places.

The sink is usually a cleanup bottleneck. The sink should be scoured and washed at the end of each class period; jars, bottles and pans must be washed and returned to their proper places; paper towels and rags used in the cleanup must be put in their proper receptacles.

To accomplish all this, a cleanup time at the end of the class period needs to be scheduled daily—five to ten minutes depending on the amount of dirt involved, the length of the period, the age of the group, and so forth. Pupils can take care of the cleanup from grade 1 (before the ending of the first year) through the senior high school. If this is done systematically, one does not have to worry too much about the neatness aspect of classroom management.

Seating Arrangements

Because a well-defined art program demands flexibility in the curriculum, flexibility in seating arrangements is necessary. In the newer schools movable furniture is usual. A variety of furniture is available for the art room in either the elementary or the secondary school. Many schools prefer large tables, seating four students, with drawing "horses" and other drawing and crafts furniture as adjuncts. Of course, there are still schools having rows of screwed down seats.

Should the latter be the case in the school in which you find yourself a teacher, the rule of thumb is to seat the smaller children near the front of the room and the taller children towards the back. The exception to the rule are those children with sight and/or hearing difficulties.

If tables and chairs are used, the same general rule is followed. The taller children are seated toward the back of the room, except as there are sight or hearing problems in the room.

Regardless of the scheme used, each pupil needs to have an assigned place. This is necessary for ease and speed in taking the daily attendance. Assigned seats also enable the teacher to become more easily acquainted with the pupils in the various classes.

Seats need to be sized to the pupil. Within each class the height of the students will vary widely, some short, some medium, some tall. Because of this, short children need to be seated on chairs and at tables that will enable them to be comfortable at their work—chairs that enable the feet to touch the floor and tables that are low enough to permit work with ease and without strain. The same principle is applied to taller children.

Taking Attendance

All schools insist that attendance be taken in each class. At times this matter is regulated by state law; the attendance register is a state register. In other places the attendance is kept and recorded by a school attendance clerk. For ease in taking attendance each student should have a permanent seat in the room in relation to other students and their places, and this should be indicated on a seating chart. By quickly glancing at the seating chart the teacher can tell who is not present.

It is possible in the upper elementary grades and the secondary school to have student monitors take the attendance daily, thus saving the teacher's time so that he can devote more time to teaching.

Pupils who are absent one day must present an excuse or admittance slip on their return. This is important for two reasons. The school authorities are then certain that the parent knows of the pupil's previous absence, and in the case of absence because of illness, the school authorities are sure that the pupil is physically well and has been admitted officially by the school physician or nurse.

Control of Student Movement

Unless the teacher has control of pupil movement within as well as without the classroom pandemonium prevails.

Students within the classroom need to know, as soon as possible after meeting you for the first time, the latitude which they have in moving about the room. Because of the very nature of the art program, it is important to have a certain amount of freedom for students within the classroom. However, freedom does not mean license.

To some extent moving around the classroom depends on the age group and the standards of the school. Usually, the older the group, the more freedom can be allowed the students to move around when necessary. Of course, the size of the group is a determinant too.

In moving from the room, again the age of the group, its size, and school tradition must be considered. In the case of older students, individuals are allowed to leave the room with permission. Many schools have a "pass" system by which the student who is not in class must have a pass signed by a teacher permitting him to be in the hall or in other designated places. Students should never be permitted to enter another room in which a class is in session unless the situation is urgent. And, of course, there should be no loitering in the halls to disturb other students and teachers.

With smaller children, movement from the room for recess is usually accomplished in a relaxed manner under supervision of the teacher. While such a duty is not a usual one for the art teacher, you should know how these things are accomplished should you, on occasion, be charged with it.

Moving, in cases of emergency, must be accomplished with dispatch, in order, and under supervision. Such movement is every teacher's business.

Always know the shortest, fastest, and approved route to leave the classroom and the building in case of fire, explosion, or other disaster. Be sure to know the standard procedure to be followed in the school where you teach.

Finally, be sure that the class is ready to leave the room when the period is officially over. Time must be allowed for the student to get from one class to another so that he can arrive at the second classroom within the time limits prescribed by the school. Whatever else you do as a teacher, be sure that the classroom is as you wish it to be before you release the class from your control.

Oftener than not your classroom will be used period after period by large numbers of children, and many times by several other teachers as well as yourself. Keeping the art laboratory neat and clean is of the utmost importance from a management point of view, from the standpoint of teaching, and as a consideration for the welfare of others. The teacher cannot start this type of housekeeping and teaching too early.

Arrangement of Special Equipment

The art program, because of its flexibility, needs a variety of specialized equipment. Much of this equipment needs to be grouped for efficiency of use. For instance, electrical equipment needs to be grouped close to an electrical outlet.

In these days of well-equipped art laboratories, there is usually a potter's wheel, an electric kiln, a wedging board, along with clay storage bins, damp cabinets, and storage shelves for glazes. Because all this material and equipment needs to be close at hand and because of the natural debris that this type of activity creates, materials for clay work need to be carefully grouped for efficiency and for a minimum of inconvenience.

Drawing and drafting equipment needs to be placed together because of the similarity of use. Drafting tables, drawing "horses," tote trays, drawing boards, easels, and similar equipment need to be located near the best natural light in the room.

Tool cabinets, crafts benches, and items like buffers need to be placed near electrical outlets for power and near gas outlets for a source of heat for such processes as soldering.

All arrangements of this sort should be made so that there is adequate traffic space, adequate natural and artificial lighting in the work areas, and with an eye to safety.

Stress should be placed on the adequacy of storage facilities. Storage space for standard bulk supplies, both flat and three dimensional, needs to be sufficient and away from constantly used areas. Shelving for bulk storage, i.e., poster paints, inks, crafts materials, is imperative. Large drawer space for flat storage of paper and boards of different types is also a necessity.

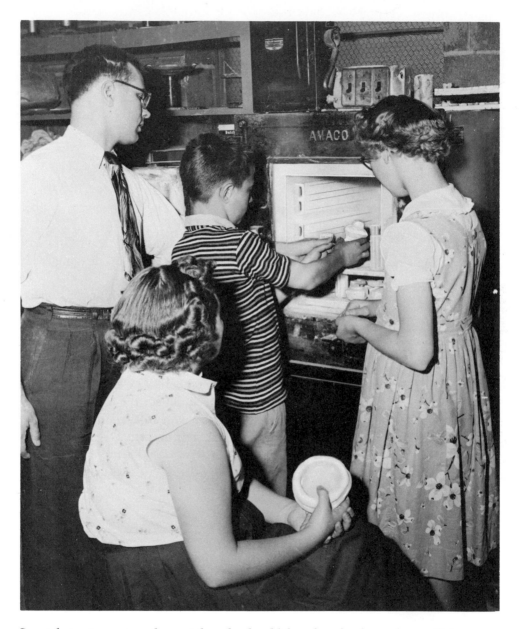

Special equipment and special tools should be placed where they will be most effective and should be cared for.

The most important storage facility, however, is that for the safekeeping of student work in process or completed. Both open shelving and flat storage areas are necessary; this storage must be clean, dry, and away from the prying hands of other students so that under all conditions student work will be kept safely.

Assistance for planning the layout of an art room is readily available through the engineers of the several manufacturers of art, drafting, and crafts furniture, and through the facilities of the state department of education and the chief of art education for the state in which you teach.

Special Problems in the Elementary School

In many instances the art teacher working in the elementary school situation carries on the art program in different rooms; there is no art room. This means that the art teacher can do one of two things: Either he can carry all materials and equipment with him from room to room, or he can store some of the essentials in each room in which he teaches. If at all possible, the latter is the more desirable way of handling the situation. Such things as rulers, scissors, erasers, crayons, and so forth can be kept in each classroom by the grade teacher. Otherwise, the art teacher wastes time by having to go back to the storage room before each class.

Distribution and collection of materials and supplies is an important part of the teaching process in the elementary school. The teacher needs to know when to pass out the materials and when to collect them so that pupils will both pay attention to directions and still have adequate time to work in the classroom. The zeal with which smaller children start an activity usually means that they must have few things to distract their attention when the art teacher is giving directions and vital information. When the art teacher has completed his motivation and directions, materials and equipment are then made available to pupils.

A similar situation prevails at the close of the art period when pupils want to keep on working past the end of the art period. The art teacher has to call a halt so that materials can be put away, the classroom can be cleaned up, and the pupils can get ready for the next part of their school day.

Special Problems in the Secondary School

In the junior and senior high school there is usually an art room in which the art teacher holds forth. If there is no room planned for the art teacher, perhaps space can be found. A teacher in a southern city found a storage room next to the coal cellar of the junior high school. After negotiations, she was able to get some repair work done and turn it into an acceptable art room. In such a room all art materials and equipment are stored or have their proper places.

The cleanup part of the class period is of particular concern in the secondary school because of the wider variety of materials used and the more complex processes in which pupils engage. Most art teachers find it advantageous to make students responsible for securing their own tools and equipment when starting their work without waiting for the teacher's permission. At the close of the class period sufficient time must be allowed for all the materials, equipment, and projects to be returned to their rightful place. The pupils also have to have sufficient time to make themselves presentable for their next class.

In cases where a variety of crafts materials and equipment are to be used, it might be well to assign students to spend a portion of time checking tools and materials in and out. Art teachers can probably learn much from industrial arts teachers as to how this can best be done. A tool crib is one answer, display panels which can be locked is another. But since each situation is peculiar unto itself, the teacher will probably have to develop his own system and arrangements.

Summary

In this chapter we have looked into some of the things which indicate the importance of classroom management as an indispensable factor of good teaching. Among these items are the physical characteristics of the classroom—temperature and ventilation conditions and lighting—neatness, seating arrangements, checking daily attendance, control of student movement during school hours within and without the classroom, and the arrangement and care of special equipment and materials.

Each of these areas has an important bearing on the effectiveness of the teaching process. Even though some of the items discussed seem to be trivial, one cannot be too careful in the management of the classroom because so much depends on the correct place and function of materials and equipment. In time, after some experience, most of the things discussed will become automatic so that almost no thought needs to be given them. It is wise to check yourself occasionally, even when you have become a seasoned teacher, so that you are always sure things are right.

For Further Reading

Association for Supervision and Curriculum Development, *Creating a Good Environment for Learning,* Washington, D. C.: The Association, 1954 Yearbook.

Mursell, James L., *Successful Teaching,* New York: McGraw-Hill Book Co., 1946.

For Further Thinking and Doing

1. After observing an elementary and a secondary art class, list the management problems which each level has. List the ways in which these problems are solved by the teacher and by the students.
2. Make a list of the routine duties and actions of the art teacher during one class period.
3. In conference with other student teachers list the ways in which student movement is controlled by students themselves, by teachers, and by the administration.

Discipline:
How to Get It, How to Hold It

"THE immediate objective of school discipline is to maintain effective work conditions."[1] This is quite a change from the historic attitude that it is important to have "discipline" so that students will do what they are told, and so that there will be "order" in the classroom as a result. Today, discipline passes under several different names, perhaps because of the stigma of the rod as a means of enforcing compliance to the will of the teacher and the association of this kind of treatment with the word discipline. Umstattd calls it "pupil adjustment."[2] Grimm and Michaelis call the process "guiding pupil behavior."[3] Regardless of the terminology used, the beginning teacher of art must realize that maintaining control for the best possible classroom climate is most necessary for successful teaching.

Most authorities conclude that there are two major sources which cause disruption of the classroom and establishment of a poor learning climate. Grambs and Iverson refer to these as "teacher-caused" and "student-caused" sources of discipline problems.[4] The former indicates a lack of understanding of teaching and social skills and lack of a thorough knowledge of the subject being taught. The latter is the set of conditions which influence student behavior.

Concerning success in the problem of discipline, one author says: "We can give you principles, cautions, devices, and techniques, but we cannot give you a money-back guarantee."[5]

[1] Harl R. Douglas and Hubert H. Mills, *Teaching in High School* (New York: The Ronald Press Company, 1948), p. 103.

[2] J. G. Umstattd, *Secondary School Teaching* (3d ed.; New York: Ginn & Company, 1953), p. 77.

[3] Paul R. Grim and John U. Michaelis, *The Student Teacher in the Secondary School* (New York: Prentice-Hall, Inc., 1953), p. 261.

[4] Jean D. Grambs and William J. Iverson, *Modern Methods in Secondary Education* (New York: William Sloane Associates, 1952), pp. 309-328.

[5] Grambs and Iverson, *op. cit.*, p. 267.

Discipline means many things. It may mean good working relationships if good motivation has been established.

Conditions Influencing Student Behavior

Even though they are not apparent, the beginning teacher must understand that there are many things which can cause discipline to collapse in his classroom. Many of the contributing factors seldom, if ever, come to the surface. All that the teacher knows is that something has gone wrong. It then becomes the job of the teacher to play detective, and find out the underlying cause of the behavior pattern of the particular child who has gotten out of line. The best way to start is to use the resources afforded by the school itself: records in the main office, the health office, those kept by other teachers and counselors, information reported by social agencies, social workers, juvenile authorities, and so forth. But what are some of the conditions outside the school which influence behavior patterns?

HOME. Since the pupil is under the influence of the home and his family for most of his waking hours, the home and family are bound to have an impact. Quite often serious disturbances in the behavior pattern can be traced to a disrupted home. Divorce, separation, and marital incompatibility are major causes for serious disturbances. Socially unacceptable parents (drunkards, criminals) can build up complexes in a child which cause his attitudes and behavior. Being one of several children in the home, all of whom are brighter or more talented than our student, can be the cause of the "I don't give a hang" attitude, especially when high goals are set for the student. Coming from a so-called "foreign" family, or a family of another race, may make it extremely difficult for the child to adjust satisfactorily to the school situation.

COMMUNITY. The community which cares little for the future of its junior citizens often is the breeding ground of maladjusted children in school. This does not have to be the entire town or city but a section of it, a neighborhood. Slums, poor recreational facilities, corrupt officials, such as juvenile authorities and policemen, open vice, and corruption peddled on every street corner and each pool hall all make for the establishment of undesirable attitudes and behavior patterns.

PEER GROUP. Low morale in the various groups, organizations, clubs, and so forth to which the child belongs is a major cause in the conditioning of behavior. When individuals are dissatisfied, they seek the companionship of similar individuals. Thus is the gang formed and thus is the behavior conditioned. If the behavior pattern of the group is not checked, the eventual results could lead to crime and imprisonment. Since satisfaction is achieved by belonging to the group, the individual conforms to its accepted patterns of behavior regardless of the values inherent in such membership and conduct.

SOCIAL AND ECONOMIC STATUS. The social and economic status of the child is often a determinant of his behavior. Deep-seated feelings in the community against the "haves" or the "have nots" cause certain students to be outcasts because they cannot belong to the larger groups on the basis of wealth or social position, regardless of which extreme of the scale they fall into.

The author knows of a boy whose foreign-born father was a day laborer in a wealthy community. All of his classmates had access to, or owned in their own name, smart automobiles. This was the basis of acceptance in the group. The boy could not get a date for a dance because he didn't have a car, couldn't afford a tux, and so forth. He therefore withdrew into himself, becoming a very shy boy, "queer" to his classmates.

MENTAL MATURITY. Frequently, the pattern of behavior is determined by the mental maturity of the individual. The pupil of low mentality often cannot distinguish between proper and improper behavior and is frequently the tool of more mentally mature children, open to their suggestions and willing to be "egged on" for the purpose of landing in the spotlight and being accepted. Douglas and Mills indicate that many of the problems of discipline arise among children of high intelligence. "If the school situation fails to present a challenge for the bright child to exercise his mental abilities, boredom and restlessness may cause him to seek outlets for his power in undesirable overt behavior."[6]

SOLVING BEHAVIOR PROBLEMS. We have discussed a few of the more common, underlying factors which cause pupils to adjust to the world in which they find themselves, in their own way. To list all possible factors would take several volumes and would then not cover all the complexities into which one travels when he is seeking answers to psychological problems. The conditions mentioned, however, can manifest themselves in boisterousness, cheating, depending on others to solve problems, open hostility (to other students or the teacher), refusal to obey reasonable requests of the teacher, refusal to do homework or assignments, impudence, "practical" jokes, and so forth. These are student-caused discipline problems which relate directly to the student and his background conditioning.

Perhaps generalized information found in the various offices of the school will not be of much help to you in cases where the pupil is *quite* a discipline problem. In that case, as a beginning teacher you will have to go further to seek help and information. You must realize that evidence of such disturbance in a personality is an indication that the trouble is deep-seated. Such a situation may call for expert assistance from the school psychologist, and perhaps even psychiatric help. Many schools today secure such help for children much as they do dental and medical care. Perhaps the trouble only seems to be severe, and all that is needed is some simple medical or dental attention. At times defects in sight and hearing can be the cause of discipline problems. At any rate, a thorough physical examination is indicated in all real serious disciplinary cases. The facilities of many community agencies, such as the church, Boy and Girl Scouts, juvenile courts, recreation departments, and the Y.M.C.A., Y.W.C.A., and Y.M.H.A. with their counseling and athletic programs may be of help. The pupil will never improve until an attempt has been made to determine the difficulty, and work with him is begun.

TEACHER AND BEHAVIOR. "Teacher-caused" discipline problems relate directly to the ineptness of the teacher in social as well as teaching skills. Being impolite, rude, inconsiderate of the feelings of others, being too familiar with pupils, or showing favoritism and discrimination are problems encountered by teachers who lack the social skills or are unable to get along with others.

[6] Douglas and Mills, *op. cit.*, p. 108.

Lack of concern for the physical comfort of the student, careless classroom procedures, making poor assignments (too vague, too difficult, too simple), poor classroom delivery, harsh voice, poor use of equipment, lack of motivation —these are all examples of lack of teaching skills on the part of the teacher. The teacher who rules with an iron hand, maintains discipline by threat or retribution, and shows a lack of leadership is borrowing discipline problems. This is the negative statement of the problem. There is a positive statement as well, a statement which should insure a minimum of disciplinary problems in the classroom. One should realize, because of individual differences, every teacher will have discipline problems to cope with on occasion.

Positive Approach

There are many devices, rules of thumb, and techniques which could be listed under such a topical heading. Some of the more important ones are set forth as a guide. Experience will teach you many more and many variations of those listed which will help in specific situations.

PUNISHMENT. Mete out punishment for individual infractions to specific students. As Gilbert and Sullivan once said, make the punishment fit the crime. Prior to assigning the punishment, be sure to hear all sides of the case and make sure that the student is actually guilty. Otherwise, forget it. Speak to the student in private, not before the entire student body. Let the student keep his self-respect in such circumstances.

Whatever the discipline problem, try to handle it yourself. This is part of your job, your responsibility. Should you be unable to cope with the situation, the school usually has procedures set up to handle such emergencies. One elementary school with which the author is familiar has the policy of sending the "bad" boys and girls to the office of the principal. After a pep talk by this individual, the student is told to "assume the angle," and he is paddled on the rump the number of times commensurate with his "crime." A secondary school in the author's experience had a full time man on the faculty who was "dean of boys" and a woman who was the "dean of girls." Discipline cases a bit out of the ordinary were to be sent by the teachers to the two specialists who used the detention halls and expulsion as the techniques of punishment. One girl in this system was "sentenced" to remain in detention hall for an hour after school for 45 school days. One wonders at this kind of punishment and what effect it has on the pupil, except to heighten resentment toward the "dean of girls" and the school in general.

Experience shows that there are always plenty of glass jars and bottles which need washing out, drawing boards which need sanding, desks and tables which need to be scrubbed and waxed—tasks which offenders can do. The pupils who do jobs of this sort seldom repeat infractions.

PLANNING. Plan to the maximum in the presentation of a problem. Make the material interesting. Use as many varied techniques for teaching as possible appropriate with the problem: demonstration, visual and audio aids, examples of the completed project, and so forth. The students should be included in the planning phase if at all possible. The students then have a vested interest in the activity. Motivate!

MANAGEMENT. Include the students in the scheme of classroom management. This is especially true in the art room. Students can be assigned as monitors to distribute materials, equipment, and work. If a tool room is in the picture, students can run this phase of the activity. Others can take care of the cleanup. The author has run a complete art program with students taking care of most of the management under the direction of a student foreman. An attendance clerk (or some other such title) can check the daily attendance. All of this kind of help creates a sense of responsibility in the students, teaches democracy in practical application, and leaves the teacher free to give maximum help to individual students and groups.

CLIMATE. The personality of the teacher can do much to minimize discipline problems in the art classroom. Be cheerful, courteous, friendly. Be able to give a joke—and take one. Respect the students and they will respect you. Good teachers have found that an informal group accomplishes more and better work than other arrangements could possibly do. A moderate amount of talking and noise lessens tensions and contributes to the casual atmosphere or climate of the class. In several situations the author has had a radio or a record player available for the use of the students at their convenience. This proved such an incentive that students literally fought to enroll in the art classes, the standard of work improved, and much more was accomplished.

Douglas and Mills list 37 "Don'ts,"[7] and Grim and Michaelis have listed a series of positive and negative attitudes to be remembered by the teacher.[8] These lists apply to the classroom in general, however, and may or may not apply to the art room. In the art room there is a considerable amount of mobility as contrasted to the academic classroom. Flexibility of seating and equipment is the keynote. Because of the kind of group participation usually involved in the art room, there will be more work noise than in the conventional classroom. However, the attitudes of the teacher should be the same where children are concerned, regardless of the kind of class in session.

[7] Douglas and Mills, *op. cit.*, pp. 118-119.
[8] Grim and Michaelis, *op. cit.*, pp. 284-285.

Experimentation with new materials often creates interests which absorb the pupil, thus eliminating discipline problems.

Summary

We have seen that discipline problems can be "student-caused" or "teacher-caused." If they are "student-caused," there is usually some condition which is the contributing factor to the unusual behavior. Some of these factors have been discussed in general terms. When one realizes how one can minimize discipline problems by correct approaches and attitudes toward teaching, it is easy to understand how one can maintain discipline in the art classroom by continuing techniques, processes, and attitudes used originally to achieve proper discipline. The only purpose which discipline serves in the classroom is to insure acceptable patterns in group and social living.

For Further Reading

Douglas, Harl R. and Mills, Hubert H., *Teaching In High School*, New York: The Ronald Press Company, 1948.

Grambs, Jean D. and Iverson, William J., *Modern Methods in Secondary Education*, New York: William Sloane Associates, 1952.

Grim, Paul R. and Michaelis, John U., *The Student Teacher in the Secondary School*, New York: Prentice-Hall, Inc., 1953.

Umstattd, J. G., *Secondary School Teaching*, 3d ed.; New York: Ginn & Company, 1953.

For Further Thinking and Doing

1. Request permission to visit the classroom of a teacher who has the reputation of being a "tough" teacher. List his techniques for getting and keeping discipline in his class. What special "tricks of the trade" does he employ with his students?

2. Select one so-called discipline problem in your classes and analyze it as to causes. Determine the root of the problem, how it grew, and what the possible solutions are to at least improve attitudes and situations.

3. To what degree is familiarity with pupils a cause of breach of discipline in the school in which you teach?

Aspects of Evaluation

In Chapter 5, *Planning for Teaching,* evaluation was mentioned briefly in terms of the lesson plan. This is but one small phase of the general topic of evaluation, and its use in that chapter is quite limited. Actually, in terms of student teaching, there are three different aspects of evaluation in which you must be interested, each having a somewhat different nature and each of importance. While these are not listed in order of importance, they are: 1) the evaluation of the teaching act by the student teacher, completed by the cooperating teacher and the college supervisor; 2) the evaluation of the public school art program; 3) the evaluation of the creative efforts of individual students in the art class.

A student teacher in art needs to know the techniques of evaluating the creative efforts of the child in school. In addition, the art student teacher needs to know and understand practices in the evaluation of an art program for the school; one day he will be responsible for such an evaluation. Lastly, it is important for student teachers to know how their performance is to be evaluated and the techniques which are to be used in the process.

Student Teacher Evaluation

In most colleges, universities, and art schools preparing art teachers in the United States, the evaluation of *you* as a potential art teacher starts long before you enter the classroom as a student teacher. You have had studio and methods classes in which you have had to achieve a certain standard before you are recommended for a student teaching assignment. The whole guidance program of the college is geared to ascertaining your potential success as a student teacher in art. In most instances, your advisor must sign your application for a student teaching assignment insuring that you have met at least the minimum standards set by the institution for student teaching. By this you can see that your probable success has been predicted some time prior to your appearance in the classroom.

When you become a student teacher and start performing before a class, the actual evaluation process of teaching ability starts. "In today's program of teacher evaluation major emphasis is placed on growth in the competencies that make a truly skillful professional worker."[1] The goals established in student teaching will vary from one student teacher to another. Every effort and opportunity are given to help the novice in his ability to work toward the goals established, to check his own growth and progress, to determine his own strengths and weaknesses, to learn where to receive help and assistance to achieve his goals, and to recognize his shortcomings as well as his abilities.

These criteria of student teaching can be established.[2]

1. Evaluation is an inseparable part of the on-going work of the student teacher.
2. Evaluation is cooperative and continuous.
3. Evaluation is in terms of clearly defined and cooperatively understood goals.

Because the evaluation process is a cooperative effort, all parties concerned are responsible for at least part of the evaluation. All parties referred to include the student teacher, the cooperating teacher, the college supervisor, and the college director of student teaching.

SELF-APPRAISAL. Probably the element of evaluation closest to the student teacher is that type of appraisal called self-evaluation. In this method the student teacher takes stock of his strengths and weaknesses and tries to improve when improvement is indicated. At the same time he learns to capitalize on his strengths. In order to use self-evaluation intelligently there must be competent guidance. When the student does not interpret his strengths and weaknesses well, guidance must enter the picture.

Group Evaluation—There are several techniques used in self-appraisal which lead the student teacher to see himself in the cold light of reality. One of these techniques is that of group evaluation. After a teaching performance, the group who observed the student teacher has an opportunity to appraise the teaching act. The student teacher always should have the first chance to appraise his own teaching. With the aid of his own ideas of his performance and the comments, questions, and suggestions of his fellow teachers, he begins to secure information, advice, and help which should lead to personal growth.

Personal Conference—The personal conference is another means leading to self-appraisal. When you feel the need of help or advice, it is usual to seek the counsel of the cooperating teacher or the college supervisor. In this manner

---

[1] Pearl Merriman and Gladys M. Fair, "Helping Student Teachers Through Evaluation," *Bulletin No. 2* (Lock Haven, Penna.: Association for Student Teaching, 1953), p. 1.
[2] *Ibid.*, p. 2.

Evaluation takes many forms. In this instance, it involves exhibition, one of the means of evaluation. It also involves public relations in that creative activity can communicate the programs to an interested public.

you receive a friendly professional evaluation of your work. Quite often the cooperating teacher or the college supervisor makes notes while observing you teaching. These notes later become the basis for a conference to improve the teaching act. Normally the cooperating teacher will record the good aspects of the teaching act as well as the parts which need improvement. When you realize this, there is less strain and fright on your part. Many times records of these conferences are kept as part of the teaching records. It is usual for the cooperating teacher or the college supervisor to have a conference with you as soon after the teaching act as possible, while it is still fresh in the minds of all concerned.

 Personal Diary—A third means of self-evaluation is brought about by a student-kept teaching diary.[3] A diary (sometimes called a teaching log) gives

[3] Grace S. Nugent, "Self-Appraisal in Student Teaching," *The Evaluation of Student Teaching*, 1949 Yearbook (Lock Haven, Penna.: Association for Student Teaching), pp. 115-118.

a running account and description of what has been done during the day. While the diary does not of itself point out weaknesses or strengths, it indicates happenings and observations which, when taken into consideration with other evaluations, are of value to you as well as to the cooperating teacher and the college supervisor. Each of these people are interested in how you observe and how you handle different situations so that you show a growth pattern.

Summary—The week's summary, while similar to the diary, is different enough to be classified separately as a means of self-appraisal. There are occasions when an interval of time will make a situation clearer or more meaningful as an experience. For this reason some cooperating teachers and college supervisors urge you to summarize at the end of each week's work or at the completion of the finished learning experience, in the case of art. At such a point you can see the situation as a unified whole rather than as single parts, as is the case with the diary. The weekly summary indicates where you have succeeded and where the activity was weak.

FORMAL EVALUATIONS. There is not a teacher education institution in the country which does not use some sort of formal evaluation for the student teacher. Most of the time this appraisal takes the form of a check list or a rating scale. At times the rating scale must be completed in narrative form, while at other institutions the rating scale involves circling a particular symbol or checking a certain box. Several examples of rating scales are to be found in the Appendix. One of the scales included indicates personal and professional traits which must be checked as unsatisfactory, poor, good, very good, and superior. Apparently the person doing the rating must rely on records kept during the course of the student teaching to arrive at the evaluation.

The rating scale used at Edinboro State Teachers College indicates a similar kind of evaluation with one major change. In the *Manual of Student Teaching* which explains how the rating instrument is to be used, the Director of Student Teaching has devised a statement which corresponds to each letter grade after a particular trait. The evaluator is to choose the phrase which most nearly fits the performance of the student teacher. There are twenty-five different qualities and abilities to be rated. An example is shown on page 73.

While there are many kinds of rating scales, the ones used are typical in illustration. In many instances these scales are accompanied by a written statement which acts as an enforcing agent for the evaluation effected on the rating scale. This is the trend currently. The worth of the formal rating scale is in its objectivity of judgement.

In terms of rating scales, the current practice is to award a grade based on the check marks made on the scale. It is becoming fashionable to eliminate a direct reference to a specific grade, but rather to state whether satisfactory or unsatisfactory performance in the teaching act has taken place.

---

17. ENTHUSIASM AND INITIATIVE

   A. Consistently demonstrates a contagious enthusiasm and resourcefulness in the presentation of material; is able to stimulate pupils to a high level of interest and participation.

   B. Shows ingenuity and initiative in devising means of stimulating pupils and demonstrates an interest in the activity of the class.

   C. Demonstrates an average interest and initiative in stimulating pupils on acceptable levels of achievement and behavior.

   D. Reveals little enthusiasm for the activities of the class and exercises no imagination or ingenuity in directing learning situations.

   E. Lacking in vitality and ingenuity in dealing with the learning situation.

Example of Evaluation Factor.[4]

One should be cautioned in placing all faith in an evaluation as objective as a rating scale. Bach suggests as one of the principles of use of the rating scale: "The rating scale should be used in conjunction with a variety of other appraisal instruments; it should not be used to evaluate behavior appraised more directly by other techniques."[5]

Regardless of the type of evaluation technique or instrument used, there is a fairly well-defined objective in making the appraisal. This well-defined objective is to assess your growth and success as a student teacher in art. But in other areas of evaluation in which you must be interested, the objective might not be so easily determined.

Evaluation of the Child's Experience

One of the areas where the objectives of appraisal are not so easily recognized as in the evaluation of your own performance as a student teacher is the appraisal of the art experience of the individual child. Objectives for

[4] L. W. Van Laningham, *Manual of Student Teaching* (Edinboro, Penna.: State Teachers College, 1954), p. 28.

[5] Jacob O. Bach, "A Scale for Evaluating Student Teaching," *The Evaluation of Student Teaching,* 1949 Yearbook (Lock Haven, Penna.: Association for Student Teaching), p. 131.

such an appraisal are many and varied. Erdt states the present emphases in evaluation as "building self-confidence, preserving the creative approach, adapting the interpretation to the maturity of the children, and helping them to become independent."[6]

In more general terms Douglas and Mills state the more important purposes of evaluation are:

1. Incentive to pupil effort
2. Diagnosis (including self-diagnosis) of pupil success and failure
3. Guidance and counseling
4. School records, research studies, and reports to parents and to colleges.[7]

In his comprehensive statement of evaluation in and through art, de Francesco states the general aims of evaluation as:

1. To predict the degree of achievement in art.
2. To measure progress or growth in concepts, manipulation, and control of materials, and adequacy of expression.
3. To differentiate and certificate pupils.
4. To diagnose learning difficulties, mental, physical, emotional, creative, aesthetic.
5. To diagnose defects in teaching procedure.
6. To determine possible remedial techniques and the aims of subsequent teaching-learning situations so that they may help pupils in need.[8]

Regardless of whose criteria for evaluations is used, most of them include some of the same ingredients in their statements. Erdt states one aspect of evaluation well when she says: "Art evaluation has no measuring stick except as each child is measured against his own growth, his past production, and his present realization."[9]

And this is just the point where many art educators fall down in evaluation technique. Many an art teacher has a preconceived idea of what the child's creation should look like in its final stage and how it should be appraised in comparison with the work of other children. Standards are arbitrary and evaluation procedures even more so.

As was stated in Chapter 5, in most situations the art teacher, as well as all other teachers, is usually required to give the student a grade as an evaluation of his progress. The percentage method and the letter and number marking

---

[6] Margaret Erdt, *Teaching Art in the Elementary School* (New York: Rinehart & Company, Inc., 1954), p. 211.

[7] Harl Douglas and Hubert H. Mills, *Teaching in High School* (New York: The Ronald Press Company, 1948), p. 411.

[8] I. L. de Francesco, *Art Education, Its Means and Ends* (New York: Harper & Brothers, 1958), p. 199.

[9] Erdt, *op. cit.,* p. 211.

Evaluation also means appraisal by peers. This photo shows college art students critically examining some of their own work.

systems of grading were mentioned briefly. In any of the grading systems the theoretical "best" student receives a "100%," and "A," or a "1." De Francesco asks some very pointed questions concerning the meaning of the arbitrary assignment of grades.[10] He also states three reasons for the continuance of grades being awarded on the traditional bases:

1. Education as a whole is still subject-matter-centered.
2. Parents are still insistent on knowing what their children are achieving in subject matter areas.
3. Institutions of higher education still insist on grades as objective evidence for admission.[11]

[10] De Francesco, *op. cit.*, p. 202.
[11] *Ibid.*

There are some educators who are desperately trying to break away from these requirements by other professional educators, parents, and colleges. Many communities are revising their report cards so that more personal evaluation of the work of the child based on his own abilities to achieve are possible. In many communities, such as those of the North Shore in Illinois, committees of parents and teachers have been engaged in this kind of activity.

But if evaluation is to measure growth, we must go back to part of the fourth aim suggested by de Francesco. The art teacher must understand the growth pattern of the whole child: physical, mental, emotional, creative, and aesthetic. Constant association with children and an understanding of their growth patterns will indicate that each child grows in the five areas mentioned according to his own native abilities and not according to some imposed system of evaluation.

The self-appraisal, the anecdotal report, and the conference method techniques of evaluation are used more and more today in addition to the traditional evaluation by means of grades.

The self-appraisal technique is employed advantageously at all age levels in the public school art program. The child is encouraged to discuss his work with the teacher and with other students. In this manner, and by observing other's work, he learns to appraise his own work, techniques, and materials.

In an anecdotal report, the teacher records in story form the happenings, experiences, and statements of the student and the student's reaction to other students and the teacher. These reports can be charted as to total experience or to a specific media. Usually these reports are included in the teacher's file on each student.

The conference method implies that the parents go to the school to meet the child's teacher. In the school the parents receive a verbal report supported by records dealing with the child's progress. The parents receive a complete account of the child's growth pattern and have an opportunity to question the teacher on items which are not clear.

In your reading for methods and philosophy courses as an undergraduate, you have been exposed to statements concerning the growth in the areas mentioned—the statements of Erdt, de Francesco, Lowenfeld, and others. Now in your period of student teaching you will have an opportunity to experience at first hand the evaluation of the work of children.

Evaluation of the Art Program

The evaluation of the entire art program of the system in which you teach is a big job. Not only does it include the work of the individual student and the physical plant and facilities, but it also includes the instructional program and the quality of instruction. Little will be said here concerning the

Children often evaluate their own work quite intelligently, thus pointing out how their own work may be improved.

evaluation of the total program, as you are probably years away from this kind of activity. It is mentioned here, however, as a culmination experience, building on the evaluation of individual students and their work and your own evaluation of your capabilities as a teacher. The sum total of the appraisal of all the art instruction personnel in the system will be an evaluation of the art program. You as part of the system will be part of this evaluation. The same principles apply and the same kinds of techniques are used.

Summary

In this chapter three types of evaluation have been mentioned—evaluation of you as a student teacher, evaluation of the creative efforts of the child, and the evaluation of the total art program.

The techniques of evaluation have been mentioned as self-appraisal, anecdotal report, conference method, and, of course, the traditional method of grades.

Every responsible authority indicates that the objectives of art education will determine what the art teachers seek in evaluation. It is evident that grades of one kind or another are not valid appraisals of total student growth as described by Lowenfeld, de Francesco, and others.

Evaluation is needed in the art program as much as it is in any other part of the total school program, and perhaps more.

For Further Reading

Bach, Jacob O., "A Scale for Evaluating Student Teaching," *The Evaluation of Student Teaching,* 1949 Yearbook, Lock Haven, Penna.: Association for Student Teaching.

De Francesco, Italo L., *Art Education, Its Means and Ends,* New York: Harper & Brothers, 1958.

Douglas, Harl and Mills, Hubert H., *Teaching in High School,* New York: The Ronald Press Company, 1948.

Erdt, Margaret, *Teaching Art in the Elementary School,* New York: Rinehart & Company, Inc., 1954.

Merriman, Pearl and Fair, Gladys M., "Helping Student Teachers Through Evaluation," *Bulletin No. 2,* Lock Haven, Penna.: Association for Student Teaching, 1953.

Nugent, Grace S., "Self-Appraisal in Student Teaching," *The Evaluation of Student Teaching,* 1949 Yearbook, Lock Haven, Penna.: Association for Student Teaching.

Reed, Carl, *Early Adolescent Art Education,* Peoria: Chas. A. Bennett Co., Inc., 1957.

Shane, Harold G. and McSwain, E. T., *Evaluation and the Elementary Curriculum,* New York: Henry Holt & Co., Inc., 1951.

Van Laningham, L. W., *Manual of Student Teaching,* Edinboro, Penna.: State Teachers College, 1954.

For Further Thinking and Doing

1. Make a brief report on the marking system used in your school. Contrast the basic philosophy of the system used with what has been mentioned in college education classes on the subject.

2. Determine the function of evaluation in the learning experiences of children in your school. Is it to report progress to parents, indicate strengths and weaknesses to students, or judge teaching competence? To what extent does it succeed?

3. Keep a running account of your effectiveness as an art teacher. With the evidence accumulated determine: *a)* does the same plan for action occur regularly? *b)* Do the same shortcomings reappear regularly? *c)* Is there any evidence of personal growth and development as a teacher of art?

Manners and Morals

THE manner in which you conduct yourself in the classroom, especially as a student teacher, will indicate your probable success as a member of the teaching profession. Not only must you consider total personality, but mannerisms, the use of the voice, and moral behavior are important also.

Use of the Voice

Most beginning teachers have been speaking, or at least talking, for about twenty years. But in spite of such courses as "Oral English," "Voice and Diction," and the constant use of the voice in practice, do they speak correctly?

Professor Nelson Hannay makes an eloquent plea for effective speech and states: "If you want to be effective in the personality that conditions speech, you must start by being a good animal."[1] He goes on to say that being a good animal includes correct posture, which leads to good breathing habits. Good habits of breathing in turn lead to effective speech.

Beyond the basic physical capabilities of speech, you need to develop an adequate teaching vocabulary to communicate with fellow teachers and administrators, as well as to develop a vocabulary to use with students. It is said that a good teacher needs a vocabulary of at least 30,000 words, including the special terms of the profession.

The beginning teacher usually falls into one of two traps concerning vocabulary. On the one hand, he may use the same kind of language that his professors used in college, in spite of the fact that the new teacher is dealing with children whereas the professor was dealing with adults. At times this vocabulary is used because the student teacher does not think about the situation and does not realize the limited vocabulary of his students. At other times, particularly in the high school, the beginning teacher uses an "over-the-head" approach to impress his students.

[1] Nelson C. Hannay, "The Instructor and Effective Speech," *A Handbook for College Teachers* (Cambridge: Harvard University Press, 1950), p. 145.

The second pitfall is that the student teacher, in order to identify himself with the group, will let his vocabulary literally go to seed. In this case, he most often uses slang and the vernacular in the mistaken notion that he will be accepted by students as one of the gang. Often, by the time he realizes it, and contrary to the belief that he was becoming popular with the students, he has actually lost their respect. Slang is permissible only on occasion, if it has a point and is especially colorful. In general, however, slang is to be avoided. Actually, you should be cautioned about being too colorful because it may lead to inappropriate use of language or even profanity. There is no room for profanity, in any degree, in the public schools. Usually such language is a sign of an inadequate vocabulary on the part of the person using it.

Vocabulary is probably the most immediate outward manifestation of the speech habits of the teacher. To a good vocabulary one can add other good qualities, such as resonance, distinctness, pitch, range, tempo, rhythm, emphasis, and timbre. It must be stated emphatically that good speech is important, and it is suggested that remedial measures be taken should you need help in any of the areas mentioned. To quote Dr. Hannay again, "You must train yourself with long patience in the skills that enable you to reveal your thoughts through the blended qualities of competent and appealing speech."[2]

Mannerisms

Probably each of us has little mannerisms which we use unconsciously every day. A mannerism is the use of a particular phrase of speech, the use of physical gestures while speaking, the use of other physical motions, or an affectation in dress.

Speech mannerisms vary widely with different individuals. One might be the use of the same word or phrase repeatedly. Such a mannerism may be due, in part, to speech patterns used in certain sections of the country. Several years ago the author knew a college president who used the word "ain't" continually, to the annoyance of all to whom he spoke. And this man had his Ph.D. in English.

Gestures while speaking are usually considered part of the Victorian theatre. However, there are still many people who continually make sweeping motions with the hands, pound the rostrum, or shake the finger while speaking. At times the physical aspects of speech take the form of pacing or other forms of physical activity. A teacher in a New York high school regularly put his students at ease by twirling a key ring while strolling before the class. A supervisor in the Chicago area kept his teachers in pain by cracking his knuckles. Some stroke their hair, rub their chins, and some even scratch.

[2] *Ibid.,* p. 155.

There are mannerisms which are not related to speaking that at times cause annoyance to others. Some of these have to do with personal actions while working at the desk, working in the library, and so forth. Many chew at the end of a pencil or tap the pencil on the book which they are reading. Some chew gum or the eraser on the pencil. One teacher in North Carolina constantly bounces on the ball of one foot while his legs are crossed. Many people drum their fingers on the table top while they are presumably concentrating. You have seen people with similar mannerisms. In themselves these do not amount to much and do little harm, but when they become distractions to other people, then mannerisms become important out of all proportion to the original reasons for them.

Affectations in clothing can also be considered mannerisms. This kind of a mannerism is usually more prevalent among male teachers than female. Bright socks, loud ties, Bing Crosby type sport shirts are common trademarks for some teachers. A coach in a large Southern college wears a bright red vest on campus. A teacher in metropolitan New York is classed as a "character" by his students and colleagues alike because he wears well-styled and expensive clothes . . . with his tennis shoes. A basketball coach in Illinois wears an exceptionally large diamond ring which is flashed about particularly when he is talking with his students. More is said on the subject of dress in Chapter 14, *Securing a Teaching Position*.

Your Total Personality

Psychologically, personality can be defined as an integrated group of emotional trends and behavior tendencies. This group of trends and tendencies is one of the most important factors in successful teaching. Personality includes such diverse attributes as cheerfulness, honesty, integrity, sincerity, and a sense of humor.

CHEERFULNESS. A cheerful teacher in the classroom can make the difference between student interest in school and being in school under compulsion. The impression made by a teacher who can smile on occasion is one which enables the student to smile in return. Cheerfulness in the teacher implies a bright and balanced temper; it shows itself in his face, voice, and actions. The student teacher would do well to cultivate this aspect of personality because much more can be accomplished under pleasant working conditions. This is one of the major ingredients for the establishment of a positive climate in the classroom. Cheerfulness manifests itself by a smiling "good morning, George," or the willingness to referee a recess softball game in good grace or by assuming responsibility for the decorations for the senior dance.

SENSE OF HUMOR. A sense of humor will probably pull you through more rough days than anything else. To be able to make a joke is almost an art. To be able to take one is to be an honest-to-goodness human to your class. A sense of humor is part of the ability to be cheerful. Occasionally, laughter at something that is funny is a safety valve to relieve tensions in the classroom. In practice in the classroom, it is often discovered that occasional joking with the students tends to lessen the formal atmosphere. This indicates a better climate and perhaps better relationships and better work results. But when you joke with students and things backfire, be sure that you can "take it" in good grace. Be able to laugh at yourself.

APPEARANCE. Your general appearance is important from several standpoints. Neatness is one of the important factors. There is no excuse for poor grooming; any student teacher can be neat and clean.

Young women should avoid excessive make-up. Lipstick, powder, rouge, and nail polish are permissible if not overdone. Eye shadow and theatrical make-up are not considered in good taste in the classroom. The same may be said for perfumes.

One should dress sensibly and for comfort. Young women should not wear party dresses or "spike" heels to class. Skirts and blouses or business suits are the types of clothing to wear. Flat shoes or shoes with walking heels should be worn, as you will be on your feet continually for five to six hours a day.

Young men should shave every day. Five o'clock shadow is not considered good grooming. A haircut, with regularity, will do wonders for your appearance. College men should avoid freakish tonsorial styles. Men are urged to wear jackets and ties whenever possible. Comfortable shoes are the watchword here too. Be careful about wearing very bright socks and loud neckties.

It is sometimes customary in rural areas and in some other regions to wear sport shirts open at the collar and, sometimes, no coat or jacket. The best advice that can be given is to check with the master teacher with whom you work to find out what is acceptable attire in the school in which you do your student teaching. It is suggested for both men and women that you wear some kind of protective clothing while actually working in the art room. Aprons or smocks for the women and shop coats or coveralls for the men are preferred by most experienced hands.

HONESTY. Anyone dealing with young men and women must of necessity espouse honesty. The teacher, in addition to his personal honesty, must be an example of this virtue to his students in all things. He must believe implicitly in what he teaches and in what he creates. Original thinking in his own work is important. There is no room for dishonesty or unfairness in the treatment of subject matter or in the treatment of students entrusted to his care.

This young lady is ready to teach. She is appropriately dressed, well-informed, and she has the materials and an example of the experience she will teach.

INTEGRITY. Integrity is a virtue closely akin to honesty. It has a further implication of soundness of moral judgment in dealings with others: impartiality, standing for what one believes, "professional integrity." One of the ways in which this is practiced in the classroom is to mean what you say. If the student teacher, for instance, states that anyone who cheats in a test will get a zero for his efforts, the teacher had better mean it if he hopes to have and keep the respect of his class. Honesty and integrity are virtues of a teacher's reputation which must be earned over a long period.

SINCERITY. Again, as in the case of honesty and integrity, sincerity is something which must be developed over a long period of time. The student teacher in art must be genuine in his feelings toward his subject, his students, and in his own efforts. He cannot believe one thing and teach another; this is hypocrisy. Many of our art teachers today praise the efforts of contemporary artists because they feel that this is the thing to do, regardless of their personal likes and dislikes. Just because Picasso's name is attached to a work of art, there is no guarantee of its ultimate artistic worth. Many would praise it because, to paraphrase, "Picasso can do no wrong."

If shoddy or poor work is submitted, the student teacher should deal with it in its proper relationship to the student who submitted it. Don't praise the work even if it belongs to the daughter of the president of the school board.

Human Relations

While doing your student teaching, you will have in your classes young men and women who will be close to your own age. Some student teachers have found this to be a problem because of the fact that young people are human.

It is natural for young people to find a young, fresh, pretty (or handsome, depending on the sex), neat, new teacher an important item of interest. Young women occasionally get a crush on the handsome young male teacher, and young men will begin to fall in love with the pretty young female teacher. As a result, it is not uncommon for students to offer the teacher a ride to and from school each day, to eat lunch with the student teacher instead of with schoolmates, to bring presents to the teacher, to write notes, and to display other adolescent traits.

At times students become serious in their attentions to the student teacher. This situation is generally difficult for the student teacher, especially if he is a long way from home and college, away from family and friends in a strange town. He is lonesome.

It is at this point that you must resist the temptation to "date" one of the students. Maintain a friendly student-teacher relationship, but not too friendly. Do not accept gifts or the proffered ride. Eat with other teachers and not with students. In student relations in class, do not show partiality because of personal preference. Treat students equally and you will have no problem.

Not only do you have your own personal and professional reputation to maintain, but you must also protect the moral reputation of your students and the good name of your college. Particularly in small towns and rural areas, gossip can start from an innocent occurrence. *Be Careful!*

Summary

The intention of student teaching is to provide for the beginning teacher an introduction into the profession. During this period, the future teacher has an opportunity to gain practical experience in many phases of teaching, including some of the aspects of personality development.

Some of the attributes which enhance the professional experience for the student teacher were discussed. These included a discussion of the use of the voice and proper speech habits, personality traits, mannerisms, appearance, and human relations.

For Further Reading

Douglas, Harl and Mills, Hubert H., *Teaching in High School,* New York: The Ronald Press Company, 1948.

Hannay, Nelson C., "The Instructor and Effective Speech," *A Handbook for College Teachers,* Cambridge: Harvard University Press, 1950.

Yauch, Wilbur A., Bartels, Martin H., Morris, Emmet, *The Beginning Teacher,* New York: Henry Holt & Co., Inc., 1955.

For Further Thinking and Doing

1. By observing a master art teacher make a list of the ways in which the following characteristics are manifested in the classroom: cheerfulness, sense of humor, neatness, honesty, integrity, sincerity.
2. By giving concrete examples from classroom observation, list ways in which teachers have tried to instill moral conduct in their students.
3. By observing you teach, have your fellow student teachers list mannerisms which you have while performing before a class. Of how many of these were you aware? How can you remove these mannerisms?

10

The Cooperating Teacher

Lowder, referring to the place of the cooperating teacher in the student teaching program, says: "Of all the persons in the program, the cooperating teacher is undoubtedly the most important, for it is he who is responsible for guiding the student teacher each day during his off-campus experience."[1] This position is easily recognized when one understands the great responsibilities of the cooperating teacher.

Responsibilities

The responsibility of the cooperating teacher (sometimes called a critic teacher or a master teacher) is two-fold in nature. In the first place, since he is a regularly employed teacher in the school district, he has all the normal responsibilities of a classroom teacher, including the responsibility for the growth and the welfare of the pupil. He manages the classroom, establishes the routines, keeps records, organizes the courses of study, and performs all the duties of an interested, successful teacher.

Secondly, the cooperating teacher is responsible for supervising the activities of the student teacher in such a way that optimum growth results, that the task of the student teacher is a challenge to him but still within his reach.

Van Laningham lists twelve responsibilities of the cooperating teacher.[2] Briefly stated they are:

1. Orient the student teacher with physical plant and school and classroom regulations.
2. Induct him into the program.
3. Aid him in planning.
4. Determine time for him to assume teaching responsibilities.

[1] Paul A. Lowder, *The Program in Off-Campus Student Teaching* (Albany: New York State College for Teachers, 1953), p. 45.
[2] L. W. Van Laningham, *A Manual for Student Teaching* (Edinboro, Penna.: State Teachers College, 1954), p. 4.

5. Advise him of teaching techniques when appropriate.
6. Demonstrate effective teaching techniques.
7. Assist him in understanding pupil growth and development.
8. Assist in locating source material.
9. Guide him in evaluation of his own strengths and weaknesses.
10. Observe him teaching.
11. Give him an opportunity to assume full classroom duties.
12. Determine when the privileges of teaching are to be withheld because of unprofitable experiences for the class.

You can readily see the tremendous responsibility which the cooperating teacher has to the student teacher. The final and ultimate responsibility of the cooperating teacher is to evaluate the quality of performance of the student teacher both in and out of the regular classroom hours. This usually means the assignment of a grade in cooperation with the college supervisor of student teachers. More has been said on this subject in Chapter 8.

Qualifications of the Cooperating Teacher

The qualifications for cooperating teachers vary more widely in the United States than does certification for the area in which they labor. While it cannot be determined that the several states have specific qualifications for employment, all institutions which do employ cooperating teachers try to secure

The art director shares in overall planning with staff associates.

The art critic teacher holds group conferences with student teachers to evaluate the art program and child development.

the best qualified teachers available. One college in Pennsylvania requires that cooperating teachers "possess the Master's degree in their field of specialization, have had five or more years of experience, three of which must have been in the public schools, and be recommended by their administrators as being superior teachers."[3]

A college in New York, states similar qualifications: "at least three years teaching experience, the possession of the Master's degree or its equivalent, a college major in the student teacher's area of specialization, and evidence of professional growth through participation in the work of professional organizations or through other educational activities."[4]

Relations with the Cooperating Teacher

Your relationships with the cooperating teacher will take many forms during the time when you are working with him. At times he will be your teacher, at times confident, father confessor, parent, and many other roles. He

[3] *Ibid.,* p. 1.
[4] Lowder, *op. cit.,* p. 15.

A weekly general practicum of student teachers with their college supervisors and cooperative teachers is a worthwhile procedure.

will be able to play all these parts because he will have made it his business to find out all that he can about you. Records and information at your college will be available to him so that he can secure such information to help him in his work. He will know something of your home and community background; any previous experience with children; your special interests and strengths. This information is necessary so that the cooperating teacher can do the best possible job in helping you become a worthy teacher and in telling you how you can best work into the program in his school. Before you arrive at his school he can begin planning for your teaching experience. In addition to the records available from your college, the cooperating teacher has probably had a conference with the supervisor of art student teachers. At this meeting information usually not found in the records will be discussed. Personal qualifications, personality traits, and language habits will be part of the information discussed.

As was mentioned above, the college is always trying to secure the best possible person to be a cooperating teacher. He will have at least the minimum professional requirements, but you must remember, these are extremely high compared with requirements for certification of similar teachers in the field. In addition to these qualifications, it is important for you to know as much as you can about the cooperating teacher. What is he like? Since he is going to play such an important part in launching you on your teaching career, you will look to him for guidance, approval, help, sympathy, ideas, and criticism. Since you will work hard and long for the cooperating teacher, you need to know him. What standards does he have? What does he believe constitutes a good education for his students? What goals does he have for his class? Does he expect you to help maintain certain limits of behavior on the part of the children? Are there certain ways of working, routine, that you must fit into? Should you tell him when you feel you are ready to take the responsibility of the class? Just what does he expect of you?

Some Specifics

You should find out what the cooperating teacher is like as a person and you should let him know what you are like also. While there is a professional relationship which must be maintained, remember that you and the cooperating teacher are humans too. It is perfectly proper to relax when not in the classroom with children and even joke with one another. It has been the practice in some schools for the student teacher and the cooperating teacher to use first names in private and in situations where they are not with students.[5]

Your cooperating teacher will probably break the ice in introducing you to the rest of the faculty in the school and the administrative staff which you have probably not met. As for student-teacher planning, you will probably be invited to planning sessions with students. You will be encouraged to make suggestions and share ideas with students as well as teachers. If the cooperating teacher is the usual progressive person, you will be encouraged to use the classroom just as if it were yours, but once again, remember that you are the guest in this classroom. Help when you can with whatever you can. Take your share of the chores that are the drudgery of housekeeping.

When you need advice or help, don't be backward about asking for it from the cooperating teacher. All of us, at one time or another, have had to seek help from a more experienced teacher. You are in the classroom to gain experience. Make sure that every minute counts and is put to good advantage.

Summary

In this chapter we have briefly discussed some of the responsibilities of the cooperating teacher, the qualifications which the college finds advantageous for the cooperating teacher to have, and the relationships which the student teacher has with the cooperating teacher. The emphasis has been placed on this individual so that you can appreciate the cooperating teacher as a person and a professional colleague. Without the cooperating teacher there would be either no student teaching program or one of very poor quality. He is your guide and teacher in this very important aspect of your education.

[5] Ernest J. Milner, *You and Your Student Teacher* (New York: Teachers College, Bureau of Publications, Columbia University, 1954), pp. 11-21.

For Further Reading

Adams, R. W. and Toulouse, R. B., "State Programs for Providing Good Laboratory Facilities in Teacher Education," *Facilities for Professional Laboratory Experiences in Teacher Education,* 33rd Yearbook (Lock Haven, Penna.: Association for Student Teaching, 1954), pp. 56-100.

Burnett, L. W. and Dickson, G. E., "Cooperative Improvement of Off-Campus Student Teaching," *Journal of Teacher Education,* 1:287-90 (Dec. 1950).

Christian, E. E., "Coordinating the Student-Teaching Program from the Point of View of the Cooperating Secondary School," University of Pennsylvania Bulletin, School of Education, *Critical Problems in Education,* 49:232-9 (June 30, 1949).

Engle, Shirley and Sharp, Donald M., "The Cooperating School: Current Functions in Teacher Education," *Functions of Laboratory Schools In Teacher Education,* 34th Yearbook (Lock Haven, Penna.: Association for Student Teaching, 1955), pp. 32-60.

McGrath, G. D., "Supervisors of Student Teaching, Our Most Seriously Hampered Asset," *School and Society,* 72:166-8 (September 9, 1950).

McGrath, G. D., "Upgrading the Services of Cooperating Teachers," *Peabody Journal of Education,* 27:237-42 (January, 1950).

Milner, Ernest J., *You and Your Student Teacher,* New York: Teachers College, Bureau of Publications, Columbia University, 1954.

Lowder, Paul A., *The Program in Off-Campus Student Teaching,* Albany: New York State College for Teachers, 1953.

Permenter, J. A. and Moon, R. C., "Selection and Status of Off-Campus Supervisors," *Facilities for Professional Laboratory Experiences in Teacher Education,* 33rd Yearbook, Lock Haven, Penna.: Association for Student Teaching, 1954.

Van Laningham, L. W., *A Manual for Student Teaching,* Edinboro, Penna.: State Teachers College, 1954.

For Further Thinking and Doing

1. In conference with the cooperating teacher, make a list of the requirements expected of you during your tenure as an art student teacher.

2. Prepare a biography of yourself in narrative form which can be of use to the cooperating teacher in knowing you better. Include incidents which have had a firm bearing on your chosen profession, your philosophy of teaching, the importance of the art program to students, and so forth.

11

School and Community Relations

In general, as an undergraduate, you have secured some information about the basic structure of school organization in Education classes. But now that you are to become personally involved in a school, you must know for certain about this organization and your relationships with the various individuals who hold positions in the administrative setup. But your relationships will not be solely with the school. You will also be a member of the general community and will have relationships with individuals and organizations in the community. First, however, let us consider the relationships you will have with the school.

School Relationships

You will soon realize that some of your school relationships are quite close, while others are rather remote. You will find that your contacts with students will be the most common, of course, followed in order by associations with other teachers, the principal, and the supervisor. In addition to the professional staff you will come into intimate daily contact with the noninstructional staff. This staff includes such diverse individuals as the custodian, the bus driver, the switchboard operator, the information clerk, the secretary, the census taker, the attendance clerk, the health employee, the lunchroom employee, and the business office employee.[1]

Enough has been said in other chapters about your relationships with students. We shall concern ourselves here with other school associations with which you must become familiar.

OTHER TEACHERS. Daily you will come into contact with other teachers in the school. You will pass them in the hall, you will sit with them in the teachers lounge, you will eat lunch with them, you will consult with them concerning students and student events. You must treat these other teachers in a most professional manner, just as you wish to be treated by your colleagues. This usually means that you must show a spirit of cooperation. Help whenever

[1] Ward Reeder, *An Introduction to Public-School Relations* (rev. ed.; New York: The Macmillan Co., 1953), pp. 184-185.

you can. Help students, student groups, and teachers who are interested in specific students and student activities. In such a close professional association you must constantly be on guard against criticizing others.[2] Many times teachers are accused of being "catty" because of their personal criticisms of one another. Please consult Chapter 14, *Professional Ethics,* concerning the conduct of teachers.

Thoughtlessness on your part may cause friction in relationships with other teachers. Be punctual at meetings so that you will not keep other teachers waiting and cause them to lose valuable time. Make accurate reports the first time so that all who handle the reports can get their work done correctly and on time.

PRINCIPAL.[3] Your contact with the principal will be less frequent than with other teachers. The principal's job is to supervise instruction in his school and to administer the school and its personnel. In your relations with the principal you carry out instructions, secure help when you need it, and consult him as an advisor on courses of action to be taken in particular problems.

The principal is the administrative officer of your school. Policy statements and announcements of the Board of Education and the superintendent of schools are made by the principal and interpreted by him if necessary. The principal often makes suggestions for improving the instruction of the teacher. It is wise to try the suggestions if you have not done so before. Results should be reported to the principal, regardless of the outcome.

The so-called "chain of command"[4] includes the principal as an integral part of the "chain." As a student teacher, and later as a regular contract teacher, you must respect the position of the principal. Should it be necessary to see the superintendent for some reason, be sure to clear the appointment with the principal. Again, this is clearly a question of professional ethics. You do not go over the head of the principal for any reason.

SUPERVISOR. The art supervisor is the person on the administrative staff who is responsible for the technical operation of the art program. In anything having to do with this aspect of your job you are responsible to this person.

It is usually the responsibility of the art supervisor to construct the art curriculum, propose the names of new teachers, prepare the art budget, and buy the supplies and equipment for the program. Should you have any difficulty or question with these items you should consult the supervisor. He holds a unique place in the "chain of command" in that his position cuts across lines.

---

[2] John C. Almack and Albert R. Lang, *The Beginning Teacher* (New York: Houghton Mifflin Co., 1928), pp. 174-176.

[3] Wilbur Youch and others, *The Beginning Teacher* (New York: Henry Holt & Co., Inc., 1955), pp. 272-277.

[4] This is a saying originating in the armed forces meaning the line of succession of authority.

He is directly concerned with you as a part of the total program, and you are responsible to him. He does not take the place of the principal; he is not immediately interested in the daily attendance, class discipline, and so forth, as a principal must be.

You will find the art supervisor a sympathetic listener to your troubles, who can usually give you a big assist in your art program problems. As has been mentioned elsewhere in this book, try to solve your own problems. But when you need help, don't hesitate to seek it.

SUPERINTENDENT. The superintendent is the chief administrative officer of the public schools. As chief administrator of the schools his responsibilities lie in seven areas:

1. Organization—the establishment of the total organization of the schools; rules and regulations which govern its conduct.
2. Instructional program—the curriculum, course of study, educational objectives, measurement, and evaluation of outcomes.
3. Business administration—the bookkeeping, accounting, and purchasing procedures.
4. Personnel—the employment and assignment of teachers and other workers in the schools.
5. Plant management—the maintenance, repair, and construction of school buildings.
6. Financial administration—the setting up of the budget, the payment of bills, the total tax structure of the public school district.
7. Interpretation of the schools—the public relations program.[5]

Because of all this responsibility, the superintendent has competent assistants to help with his duties—principals and supervisors. This is the primary reason why your relations with the superintendent, when you are a regular contract teacher, will be rather remote. Usually the superintendent of a small or medium-size school district reserves the right to hire teachers himself, to promote them, and to apply salary scale and tenure principles.

When you have questions relating to these areas, you should see the superintendent. But as cautioned previously, be sure to go through the office of your building principal—the "chain of command."

BOARD OF EDUCATION. The Board of Education is the policy making group of the public schools. The board derives its authority from the people because, in the majority of cases, the school board is an elected body. In addition to being elected by the people, the board derives its power from state law.

While your dealings with the board are rather remote, you must remember that when you sign a teaching contract it is with the Board of Education.

[5] Youch, *op. cit.*, p. 271.

Noninstructional Staff

As has been mentioned previously, you will come into daily contact with the noninstructional staff. Only one member of this staff will be mentioned here—the custodian.

The custodian is probably one of the most important persons in the school as far as you are concerned. Because of the number of ways in which he can help you in being a more effective teacher, you should cultivate his friendship and loyalty.

Most generally it is the custodian who delivers materials, supplies, and equipment to your art room. If he understands how you work and appreciates your efforts as a teacher, it is more than likely that he will put forth a bit more effort to help you in unpacking materials, supplies, and equipment. When the equipment is heavy, bulky, and dirty, you will appreciate a willing hand to help install it, clean it up, and get in in running order.

The custodian is also responsible for keeping the art room clean. If he sees that you are trying to help him in this part of his job by making sure that each class cleans up as much of its dirt as possible, he will spend more time in doing a very thorough job for you. The author once received this kind of cooperation in a public high school. On an average of once every two weeks, the custodian saw to it that the art room floors were scrubbed and waxed—not just a buffing or polishing, but a real wax job. This was especially true when something special was to be held in the art room.

There are hundreds of additional ways in which the custodian can help you. In instances known to the author, he has helped in hanging exhibits; he has promoted lumber for shelves and installed them when the principal said there was no way to get them. He has made special items needed for the art program when they couldn't be secured any other way. He has produced a cup of coffee on occasions when one was desperately needed.

Because your art classes could, and possibly do, cause the custodian so many maintenance problems, it is up to you to help him as much as you can. In return you will usually find that the custodian can and will do many things for you. Cooperation is truly a two-way street.

And so it should be with your relationships with others of the non-instructional personnel—secretary, clerk, driver, and so forth. A cheerful "good morning," a genuine interest in the problems of others and in the people themselves are good ways to start your relationships on a positive road.

Community Relationships

All of your associations are not with your co-workers. You are also a member of the community and have all the normal relationships any citizen has. Some of these are with groups, others are with individuals.

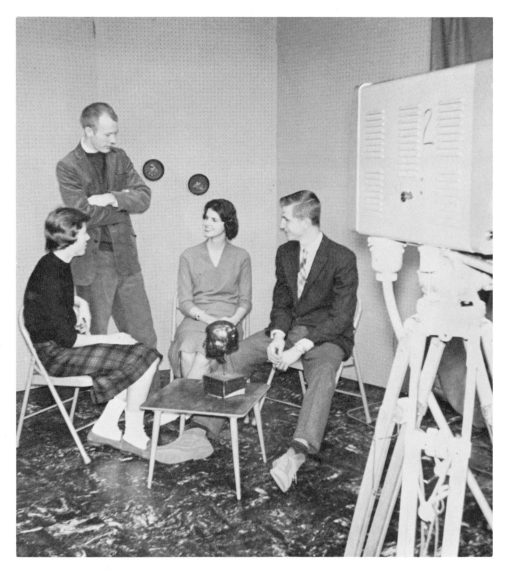

The art supervisor conducts a telecast in which art student teachers participate.

PARENT-TEACHER ASSOCIATION. The P.T.A., as it is usually called, is a community group closely allied to your profession. In many communities membership in this organization is compulsory for teachers; in others it is voluntary. As a student teacher you should attend its meetings in the school district in which you teach so that you can learn about the organization and how it works.

Originally the parent-teacher movement was locally inspired. Then it spread statewide and finally nationwide. Reeder indicates that this movement started as early as 1855.[6] The national organization started in 1897 as the *National Congress of Mothers.*[7]

The purpose of this organization is best expressed by the P.T.A. itself in its bylaws:

> *First,* to promote child welfare in home, school, church, and community; to raise the standards of home life; to secure more adequate laws for the care and protection of children.

> *Second,* to bring into closer relation the home and the school so that parents and teachers may cooperate intelligently in the training of the child; and to develop between educators and the general public such united efforts as will secure for every child the highest advantages of physical, mental, moral, and spiritual education.[8]

Contrary to the opinions of many schoolmen that this organization is meddlesome, many teachers and administrators have found it of tremendous help in solving problems of the school. The P.T.A. of Highland Park High School, Highland Park, Illinois, is especially helpful to the art department of the school through its art committee. This committee helps the art teachers select exhibitions and helps hang these exhibitions in the school hallway which was especially prepared by the committee by use of "peg-board" panels and lighting. The committee has further helped by providing insurance to cover any damage while the exhibitions are up. Another important assist from this committee was the preparation of a brochure about the art department of the school for parents, explaining the program, facilities, and the staff members.

You should be sure that you are a member of the P.T.A., first for the good that you can do for it, and second, for the good it can do you.

LABOR ORGANIZATION. It is quite possible that the teaching staff in your area will be unionized. The organization of teachers by labor unions has proceeded at a greatly accelerated pace during recent years, especially in the areas around large metropolitan communities. Usually the labor group which organizes the teachers is the AFL-CIO American Federation of Teachers.[9]

Should you become a member of a local union, this association brings you into direct contact with organized labor in your community through joint labor councils. The labor councils are groups made up of representatives of each

---

[6] Reeder, *op. cit.,* p. 143.
[7] *Loc. cit.*
[8] National Congress of Parents and Teachers, *By-laws,* Art. II.
[9] See Chapter 12, "Professional Associations."

of the local unions doing business in the particular community. Such an association will give you an opportunity to learn at first hand the problems of the working force and to lend your support to improve the status of all workers, not just teachers.

COMMUNITY LIVING. Years ago, when a teacher signed a contract, one of the contractual obligations of the teacher was to live in the town in which he was employed. Some school districts even went so far as to indicate the number of weekends per month the teacher was expected to stay in town.

Since World War II, this kind of thing has changed because of the shortage of teachers. However, Farmville, North Carolina, will not employ a teacher who does not or will not live in the community. This is but one of many examples which could be cited. It is understandable that the teacher ought to live in the community in which he teaches because so much of his professional interest is there.

When you receive your living from a particular community, it is reasonable to suggest that it is wise to do some of your shopping in the town. Granted that you might get better "bargains" in the larger city close to your town, you aren't being paid by the larger city. And you need to take into consideration the expense involved in traveling to the larger city. If it is a question of selection, then that is a different problem.

It is probably wise to affiliate with one of the local churches in the community. This is especially true if the town has a church of your denomination. At times this could be difficult, as there might not be a church of your denomination. Be realistic and realize that the chances are that you will not return to your home town as a resident. Therefore, the community in which you teach is going to be your home. By this reasoning the suggestion is made that you join a local congregation, or at least attend some church with regularity.

Get into the swing of community living by joining local organizations in which you have an interest or of which you have been a member in your home town. Fraternal organizations, such as the Masons, Knights of Columbus, Odd Fellows, Moose, Elks, usually have local organizations in the larger communities. There are always political groups, such as the Democratic Club or the Republican Club.

Many beginning teachers have probably been in the armed forces. Most communities have posts of the American Legion, the Veterans of Foreign Wars, Amvets, or some similar group. It is quite possible that the young men might be interested in joining the reserve service organizations, in many cases because of remaining service obligation time. The army reserve, naval reserve, or air force reserve have units in most areas, usually within commuting distance.

Subscribe to the local newspaper and the state magazine if you are in a new section of the country. These periodicals will keep you abreast of what is

53320

Using community resources is one way of making art live, as well as paying tribute to the local scene. Students here are sketching at the Philadelphia Zoo.

happening in the community and will offer an opportunity to learn some of the interesting facts about the community in which you teach.

Be sure to keep your credit rating as high as possible. Accomplish this by doing business with a local bank as a starter. When you receive monthly bills for milk, for fuel, or for charge accounts from local stores, be sure to pay the bills promptly. Because of your more or less public position, you cannot afford to let bills drift from month to month without payment. Teachers as a group have excellent credit ratings because of the care they take in seeing that their obligations are met on time. Don't damn the rest of the profession because of your shortcomings.

Summary

In this chapter we have covered broadly your relationships within the school and within the community. Mention was made of the "chain of command" and your relationship with people in this line of authority. Mention was also made of your living in the community as a citizen: your church affiliation, social and fraternal membership, labor relations, political activity, business connections, and school-community groups such as the P.T.A.

Honesty, integrity, understanding, and sobriety in your manner of living in the school and the community are important. Cooperation and understanding are probably the most important traits which you can exhibit.

As a student teacher, you should investigate school and community relationships as a learning device. Participate in community activities if at all possible for immediate as well as future reference.

For Further Reading

Almack, John C. and Lang, Albert R., *The Beginning Teacher,* New York: Houghton Mifflin Co., 1928.

Moehlman, Arthur B., *School Administration,* rev. ed.; Boston: Houghton Mifflin Co., 1951.

Reeder, Ward, *An Introduction to Public-School Relations,* rev. ed.; New York: The Macmillan Co., 1953.

Shane, Harold G. and Youch, Wilbur A., *Creative School Administration,* New York: Henry Holt & Co., Inc., 1954.

Youch, Wilbur A. and others, *The Beginning Teacher,* New York: Henry Holt & Co., Inc., 1955.

Stearns, Harry L., *Community Relations and the Public Schools,* Englewood Cliffs: Prentice-Hall, Inc., 1955.

For Further Thinking and Doing

1. What kind of relationships exist over a period of a month between teachers, between teacher and principal, between teacher and supervisor, between teacher and superintendent?

2. Learn to know the people with whom you work. Maintain a positive approach with them. Recognize good intentions in people. Observe other teachers. Take advantage of opportunities for contact with parents.

3. As a teacher, what kinds of relationships do you have in the community?

4. Using a map of the town, look over the community to learn of the social and economic environment of the neighborhoods from which children come to your school.

12

Professional Associations

WHEN one is a teacher, he has definite obligations beyond contractual commitments—to himself, his community, his school, and his students. These obligations are many and varied and are principally in the form of leadership in community activities and participation in professional organizations and groups.

As an art teacher, you have a dual purpose in these activities: One is primarily "professional" while the other is more or less creative. It is your duty to become a leader in art activities in your community, to link, as it were, these activities with the school community in which you serve. You can be expected to show a participating interest in the local amateur art group. This kind of activity could well be the center of your continued interest as a producer of art. Remember what has been said before: You are an artist as well as a teacher.

Art Education

At this point in your career you probably realize that art teachers the nation over have banded together at various instructional levels because of their mutual interest in problems peculiar to art education specifically and education generally. Should you work in a large community, there will probably be a local group of art teachers who have organized to further the ends of art education in the community.

Very often the meetings for this type of group take the form of workshops, as in the case of Erie, Pennsylvania, where the teachers explore new or unfamiliar media and techniques. Teachers, supervisors, or specialists in the field who have developed new or improved ways of doing things present these techniques to other teachers who meet once a month on a voluntary basis. Even though the attendance at these meetings is voluntary, the number present at the meetings averages forty.

Still other groups, such as the one in Highland Park, Illinois, have problems of program coordination and curriculum on which to work. In this community there are three separate and complete elementary school districts which all send graduates to the one township high school. There is a great need for curriculum planning and coordination of effort when so many parts eventually make up the whole.

Other groups get together weekly or biweekly to work in different media. One such group in the midwest meets weekly in one of the church basements to paint from a model. None of the teachers could afford a model themselves, but together they can continue their professional interests in painting, whatever the style they pursue individually.

While the area around Chicago is quite densely populated, the art teachers in the area from Waukegan to Gary have a group known as the "Around Chicago Art Educators." This group meets monthly for lunch and has wonderful programs which a smaller group could not afford financially. Speakers of national and international reputation have been on the program of this group.

Smaller groups are organized on a county or area basis primarily because of numbers. Groups in smaller communities are usually ineffectual because limitations of population mean fewer art teachers.

As a student teacher, or as a full-fledged member of the profession, you should join one of these groups in order to help when you can and at the same time to learn from more experienced hands.

STATE GROUPS. Most states in the United States have some type of art education group at the state level. At times this group is actually a part of the state teachers association, as is the case in New York state, while in other places the art education group is independent, as is the case in Illinois. Many of these groups print interesting and informative articles in their publications and newsletters. Most of the time these publications can be of great help to you as an art teacher. Newsletters which inform teachers of meetings, exhibitions, and important happenings are quite common. New personalities and controversial issues are brought to the attention of the area teachers.

Not quite so common is the yearbook type of publication issued by several state organizations. For a period of several years, those issued by the Illinois art educators have been outstanding contributions to the literature in the field. Publications are important because the latest developments and research are presented and discussed for the classroom teacher. This kind of activity would not be possible if it were not for such groups which have organized and can support such an activity financially. The annual meetings of these state groups are usually an inspiration. Well-known leaders in the field demonstrate materials and processes, lecture on important topics, or talk with smaller groups using the panel or round-table discussion method.

REGIONAL ASSOCIATIONS. Next, beyond the state level, come the regional associations. There are four of these in the United States: the Eastern Arts

President Lindergreen of E.A.A. makes a presentation in New York. Prominent art leaders are in background.

Association, the Western Arts Association, the Pacific Arts Association, and the Southeastern Arts Association.

The Eastern Arts Association is made up of members from the New England and Middle Atlantic states. This is the largest single regional association from the standpoint of membership.

The Pacific Arts Association draws its membership from the Pacific coastal area and the Rocky Mountain states.

Eighteen states, from Ohio to Colorado and from Minnesota to Texas, make up the area of the Western Arts Association. This is the largest single region in size and the oldest of the four in service.

The Southeastern Arts Association comprises the states in the southeastern section of the United States, starting in Virginia and ending in Louisiana.

It is the purpose of each of these groups to function as a regional association of state groups and to accomplish tasks on this level. Because of the larger areas, there are more possible members to do more and larger jobs. For some time, at least two of these groups have been promoting research in art education on a basis which neither a state nor a local group could possibly accomplish or afford. Each regional association publishes a monthly bulletin which is one of the few current contributions to the literature of art education. Specialized phases of art and art education, calendars of events, and reviews of books and visual materials are carried in each issue. Biennially, these organizations hold regional conventions which draw attention to the problems of the profession on a regional basis. These conventions provide an opportunity to catch up on the latest information in the field; give the teacher a chance to see new and improved materials and techniques introduced and demonstrated; afford the possibility of enjoying the cultural offerings of a larger metropolitan area in a distant section of the region; and make possible consultation with others in the same branch of the profession in a larger area than a state or local group.

NATIONAL ART EDUCATION ASSOCIATION. The national organization, the National Art Education Association, is relatively new, having been established in its present form in 1947. This association is composed of the membership of the four regional association affiliates, and is a department of the major professional organization, the National Education Association. While a comparatively young organization, the NAEA has already made significant contributions to the field of art education by means of its biennial conferences and a most professional yearbook. A monthly publication, *Art Education*, focuses attention on problems in art education on the national scene.

A major contribution of the organization is the sponsorship of the International School Arts Exchange in cooperation with the American Red Cross. The most recent figures available indicate that since 1946 a total of 45,000 pieces of school art work from American school children, grades 7 through 12, have been exchanged with other countries of the world as a result of this program. It has helped build international understanding through children's art work. This past year 3619 pieces of art work of American boys and girls were distributed to 35 different countries of the world, and we received in return 1727 paintings from 25 countries.[1]

For many years a section of the NEA was devoted to art education. But over the years this section began to include more and more that had less and less to do with art education specifically. To bring the field of art education into line with other areas in education several leaders in the field, notably Dr. Edwin Ziegfeld of Columbia and Dr. I. L. de Francesco of Kutztown, working with the permanent staff of the NEA, brought into being the present organization in 1949. While the National Art Education Association is a department of the NEA, with offices in Washington, it is virtually autonomous in handling its own affairs.

[1] National Art Education Association, *Art Education*, IX, No. 7 (November, 1956), pp. 12-13.

Exhibitions of materials and equipment for a good art program are often available at regional and national meetings.

Membership is through the four NAEA affiliates; that is, if a person from New York state wishes to belong to the national association as a regular member, he must first join the Eastern Arts Association, the regional organization which embraces New York. His membership in NAEA is then automatic.

Education Associations

The art teacher should not forget, however, that he not only has an obligation to participate as a member of a pertinent organization in his specialized field of art education, but there are also professional teachers' groups with which he should affiliate.

LOCAL AND STATE EDUCATION GROUPS. Most large communities have branch groups of the state teachers organization. Usually by joining the local group, the teacher also belongs to the state organization. Both the local and the state groups are furthering the cause of education by improving teaching standards, increasing financial assistance, and improving the physical requirements of a sound educational system. At the same time, compatible with these purposes, the associations are improving the lot of the teacher in all fields. Such things as state salary schedules, retirement systems, tenure laws all stem from the very active legislative work of committees and the general membership of these groups. Several state organizations employ legal counsel for members in tenure cases and in other matters where legal advice and assistance are needed. Each state association in the United States publishes a journal for its membership, which contains news of educational happenings and reports on important controversies, meetings, materials of instruction, and current and proposed legislation.

NATIONAL EDUCATION ASSOCIATION. The National Education Association of the United States is the organization which represents the largest number of teachers on the national level. This is a professional organization founded in 1857 and has many departments and commissions working in the interest of public education. The *Journal* of the NEA is the monthly publication which informs the membership of problems on the national level and controversies in education. Recently the problem of recruitment of teaching personnel and the lack of scientific and technical preparation has received attention in the nation's press, radio, and television largely through the efforts of the NEA. Many other current problems in education have been headlined by this association and action has been pushed thereby. One can belong to many departments of the association and secure representation in the more specialized areas: Department of Classroom Teachers, Department of Higher Education, Association for Curriculum Development, National Art Education Association, and so forth. The emphasis of all departments is on the welfare of the child in school and the professionalism of the teacher. A great number of research studies and a veritable mountain of statistics have been compiled on important educational problems. This information is available to members free or at a very modest cost.

Teachers' Unions

A different type of organization of teachers is that of the labor union variety. There are several independent teachers' unions, such as the one in Norwalk, Connecticut, not affiliated with other bodies. This organization is local in scope and is concerned with such matters as teacher placement within the system, salary increases, teaching duties, hours, and so forth. It is recognized by the Connecticut Department of Labor as a bargaining agent for the Norwalk teachers. There is also the American Federation of Teachers which is

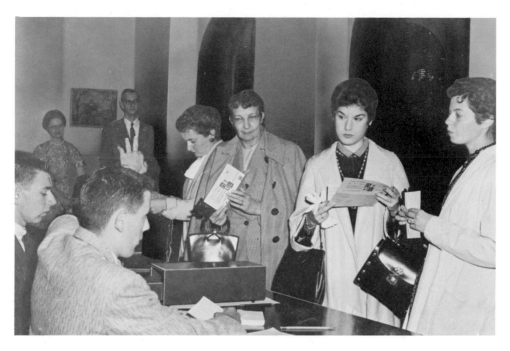

Meeting old friends and making new ones are a part of professional growth.

affiliated with the AFL-CIO. The purpose of this type of organization is mainly for the improvement of the employment conditions of the teachers who are members. Pay, promotion policy, sick leave, and general working conditions are usually the primary concern of these groups.

The first significant example of an independent teacher's organization was the Chicago Teachers Federation, organized in 1897. This organization came about as a result of a meeting held to discuss teachers' pensions. From this beginning came the American Federation of Teachers, organized in 1916, a national organization of eight locals: three units in Chicago and one each in Gary, New York, Scranton, Washington, and Oklahoma. In the introduction to the story of the AFT, the authors state that the "slogan of the Federation, 'Democracy in Education; Education for Democracy,' reveals the basic social and educational orientation of its founders."[2] The founders held the belief that American democracy could be strengthened best with the association of all workers in *all* productive occupations. They spell out simply the "crucial role" that American education must play in the maintenance of the democracy.

[2] Commission on Educational Reconstruction, *Organizing the Teaching Profession* (Glencoe: The Free Press, 1955), p. 9.

Those who founded the Federation were convinced that organizations of teachers concentrating on action were necessary, rather than the kind of past organization which was largely of the special interest groups banded together. The Federation constantly stressed "the need for classroom teachers themselves to take an active and responsible part in advancing the welfare of their profession."[3] The support which the founders wanted and needed was to be found within the framework of the organized labor union.

"This organization has consistently interpreted and promoted the interests of the teachers in the wider context of the public education program. By giving teachers a chance to co-operate with other groups in public movements to strengthen their profession, it has enabled them to win a new dignity and self-respect."[4]

Summary

Professional obligations of the teacher, while they are not contained in the teaching contract, are an important part of the teacher's life. On these obligations sometimes depends the teacher's very livelihood.

In this chapter we have discussed in general terms some of these professional obligations. It was stated that these obligations were divided into those belonging on the art side of the ledger and those on the educational side. Under the heading of obligations on the art side were included local art groups, regional and state groups, and finally national and international groups. Under the educational obligations were listed memberships in local, state, and national professional groups and in the labor organization type of group. The importance of these different groups was stressed with a view to impressing the obligations on the student teacher, in the hope that when he becomes a full-fledged member of the profession, he will join the organizations to which he feels personally related and in which he is interested.

For Further Reading

Commission on Educational Reconstruction, *Organizing the Teaching Profession,* Glencoe: The Free Press, 1955.

Douglas, Harl and Mills, Hubert H., *Teaching in High School,* New York: The Ronald Press Company, 1948.

National Art Education Association, *Art Education,* IX, No. 7, November, 1956.

Youch, Wilbur A., and others, *The Beginning Teacher,* New York: Henry Holt & Co., Inc., 1955.

[3] *Ibid.,* p. 12.
[4] *Ibid.,* p. 15.

For Further Thinking and Doing

1. Contrast the advantages of professional teachers organizations with the advantages of the teachers unions. A debate on this subject should prove interesting.

2. Discuss reasons for membership in art education organizations.

13

Continuing Professional and Creative Growth

WHEN you receive the bachelor's degree, you have just begun your career. Because you have graduated is no sign that you have "arrived" and know all the answers. If you stop growing professionally and creatively, you might just as well not accept your first teaching position.

Professional Growth

Professional growth means continued educational preparation so that you may eventually be a "good" teacher. You still have a lot to learn which isn't to be found in formalized undergraduate classes. There are several ways in which you may continue to grow professionally: formal graduate study, regular professional reading, professional assignments other than classroom teaching, professional writing, and participation in professional organizations.

GRADUATE WORK. Graduate work is the most common way to grow professionally. Not only is it beneficial to you as a teacher to take advanced work at the university and to keep up with the latest developments in the field of art education, but it is becoming a necessity in many school districts. Usually one goes to the university to work on a master's degree about a year after graduation. Most often this work is done in summers between school years. In many colleges and universities the degree can be secured in three to four summers.

It is advisable to have some teaching experience prior to entering graduate school. If you do, you will have the necessary background to more fully understand the advanced thinking concerning problems which arise every day in the classroom and the significance of these problems.

Usually a candidate can major in one of several fields, depending on the kind of degree for which he matriculates. There are five kinds of degrees in art education on the master's level: Master of Arts, Master of Science, Master of

Education, Master of Fine Arts, and Master of Art Education.[1] In one leading Eastern university which grants the master's degree, there are five distinct programs of advanced preparation in art education which the candidate may elect. These programs cover the areas of elementary, secondary, and college teaching and supervision and directorship in art. Before entering graduate school one should have in mind the kind of part he wants to play in art education and then select the college or university where there is a program which meets his needs. Don't be misled by slick university bulletins or the talk of friends about "cinch" programs when deciding at which university you will do graduate work. Find out for yourself about the school, its facilities, its faculty and program and be satisfied that they are all that you desire before matriculating.

"If the teachers college has done its job well at the undergraduate level, further teacher education should be devoted to an enrichment and strengthening of the teacher's total understanding of the responsibilities of a teacher. Except for advanced work in such fields as school administration, special education, and supervision, the teacher working on a master's degree is strongly urged to select additional credits from what are usually referred to as the 'general' fields of knowledge."[2]

"The content of the course can be related more directly to problems encountered in actual classroom situations. Courses can be chosen in terms of the specific problems of the individual teachers. Some of the most important values of summer school attendance are derived from informal discussions of teaching with teachers from other schools."[3]

If the quest is genuine, graduate work can be very rewarding in securing further knowledge of your field and in broadening your education in the general fields. In addition to progressing in your chosen profession you will be a better person and a far better teacher for your students.

PROFESSIONAL MEETINGS. As was mentioned at length in Chapter 12, the teacher has many possible professional memberships. Many professional art and educational organizations were listed and described. But listing such groups or even membership in them is not enough.

You must support actively the groups to which you belong. This means that you should be a participating member, by attendance at regular meetings and programs as well as at the annual meetings or conventions. Many times the school district will give you time off for attendance at such professional meetings

---

[1] Wellington B. Gray, *A Study of Graduate Art Education* (Unpublished doctoral dissertation, New York University, 1954), pp. 41-43.

[2] Wilber A. Youch, and others, *The Beginning Teacher* (New York: Henry Holt & Co., Inc., 1955), p. 242.

[3] Harl Douglas and Hubert H. Mills, *Teaching in High School* (New York: The Ronald Press Company, 1948), p. 566.

Meetings of art student teachers and art education majors with leading art educators provide opportunities for exchange of ideas, philosophies, and theories.

when they come during the regular school year. Some school districts even pay part of the bill, as they consider such activity as this of value to the entire school system, not just the faculty member participating. Quite often the welfare of the student, as well as the teacher, is the subject under discussion. You should have your opinion recorded. At other times new information and techniques are discussed. You, as an interested party, should be present to learn all that you can in order to become a better teacher.

Program committees are always on the lookout for interested individuals to participate in meetings. Let it be known that you are able and available as a resource person, a recorder, or a panel member of a program.

When ballots are sent to you asking for your vote on any number of possible questions, fill them out and return them as soon as you can. Should you be asked to file a report or complete a checklist, do it if at all possible. In these

Participation in local and regional curriculum discussion groups is a healthy and necessary practice.

ways you are participating as a member of a professional group, and by participating you are growing professionally as a teacher of art.

PROFESSIONAL READING. Every year there are hundreds of books published dealing with art, art education, and education. It is impossible to read all these books, not to mention the thousands of magazine articles written on every subject from "Why Johnny can or cannot read" to "Why Walt Disney should be president of the United States." One must be selective in what he reads because it is impossible to read all that is published.

As a starter, it is suggested that you read the periodicals of the professional organizations of which you are a member. Be interested in all kinds of reports and researches. Occasionally read such publications as *The Journal of Educational Research*, *The Journal of Educational Sociology*, and *School and*

Society. As for your own field of specification, don't stop with the usual art education periodicals which should include such magazines as *Art Education, School Arts,* and *Arts and Activities.* Include in your reading diet an occasional glimpse into *Arts and Architecture, Crafts Horizons, Arts, Art News,* and so forth.

For a better understanding of some of the problems of some of your students, you should occasionally read such books as *Why Johnny Can't Read, Educational Wastelands,* and other such pointed and controversial publications. Every year there are many books on educational psychology and educational sociology published. To be a better teacher and to keep up with the latest research and thinking you need to read such professional books from time to time. The state of Illinois has a novel way of encouraging this kind of reading. They list such books on a "reading circle." By reading these books one gains points, a minimum of which are needed for retention of certification.

Douglas and Mills[4] suggest a reading program for teachers. This program includes the following:

1. One good accurate daily newspaper
2. A local newspaper
3. Two weekly periodicals—one conservative, one liberal
4. One good monthly periodical
5. One digest periodical per month
6. During the year the following books:
    a) Two classics
    b) Three or four books on current problems
    c) Two or three novels
    d) One book on historical or scientific subjects

Of course this is a recommended minimum program, and any professional person should read as much of all kinds of material as time will allow.

ASSIGNMENTS OTHER THAN REGULAR TEACHING. While one fulfills his regular teaching duties each year, there are numerous other teaching assignments available. While some of these assignments are nonpaying jobs, they give you, the art teacher, opportunities for different kinds of teaching, thus broadening your experience and interests.

There are five major fields which are open, especially to the art teacher:

Adult Education—The field of adult education is a rapidly expanding field, especially in leisure time activities. Many public school districts, community colleges, regular colleges, churches, welfare agencies, and recreation boards have instituted programs in leisure time activities in recent years. Such programs include the need for art teachers to conduct art classes for the adults:

---

[4] Douglas, *op. cit.,* pp. 561-562.

drawing, painting, handicrafts. This kind of teaching offers the opportunity to teach a different age group and to teach the arts from a different approach.

Summer School—Quite often colleges, art schools, and art centers employ extra teachers for their summer programs to replace the regular faculty while they are on vacation. Again such teaching offers tremendous experience, different from that of the regular art teaching position, stimulating contacts, and the possibility of teaching in a more professional situation. Very often one can literally have a vacation while teaching during summers at colleges, art schools, and art centers in different sections of the country.

Playground Teaching—Each year more and more city schools, recreation departments, and settlement houses are providing facilities for learning during the summer. An important part of such a program includes the arts and crafts. Teaching in this type of program offers once again an opportunity for a different kind of teaching with a different emphasis. Quite often the children in this kind of program are the underprivileged who haven't had much of an opportunity for education in art. There is a tremendous personal satisfaction in such teaching, and you are learning problems of different kinds of people.

Summer Camp—Yearly there are numerous positions available for arts and crafts teachers in summer camps and dude ranches for boys and girls all over the country. Many of these positions, in addition to offering challenging teaching opportunities in yet another kind of art teaching and a summer vacation in a different section of the country, pay excellent salaries. More and more the camp positions are becoming specialized. The author knows of a girls' camp in up-state New York which employs eight counselors in the arts each summer. Their duties vary from teaching painting, crafts work, jewelry, metal work, and ceramics to stage designing.

Church School—Here is a teaching assignment which is quite necessary in our society and one which is most rewarding. Many church schools (Sunday schools, Bible schools, and so forth) need the help of the art teacher constantly, but they never seem to have enough help, and sometimes none at all. Here, once again, the emphasis in teaching is quite different and most rewarding in a personal way, not financially.

There are many other kinds of teaching positions which are available to the art teacher occasionally: art therapy for the disabled in the hospital, teaching in veterans' rehabilitation training centers, teaching mental defectives, the sightless, and the deaf, teaching in nursery schools and private kindergartens. All of this kind of teaching experience enriches the background of the art teacher and improves his professional qualifications as an art teacher.

PROFESSIONAL WRITING. There are countless opportunities for improving your professional qualifications by writing professionally on the art fields. Art education periodicals are always requesting that informative articles be submitted for publication. While the literature in art education is increasing yearly, there is always room for more good books in the field. Of course, one must have a natural talent and liking for writing or one must develop a writing technique. One must also have something to say in his writing.

The art teacher must make a contribution to the literature in the field by introducing new materials and techniques; by explaining and reporting research work accomplished; by raising important questions which need to be asked—and answered; by explaining art programs to the general public as clarification, so that the general public will better understand what is being attempted by art teachers. Photographs which explain pictorially should be used as much as possible in your writing to heighten interest and for clarification. Many publications, such as *School Arts,* depend heavily on the use of photographs in professional writing. When writing, put on paper that which you know from experience, experimentation, or study. Don't rehash other peoples' work.

Creative Growth

There are only two ways to show creative growth—study and production. One can spend the summers studying with leading artists in summer school art colonies and colleges to gain more knowledge of a technical nature. This kind of study is often needed by the young teacher just out of college where the art program has been quite basic but comprehensive in coverage. He often needs to study in depth rather than in breadth. The problem of a young teacher from Iowa is one case in point. This young lady had had but two painting courses at her college—one in oil and one in watercolor, both having to do with still life painting. She dearly wanted to paint more. What she needed was more painting, not art history, and so forth. However, there are times when study in breadth is in order. Another example in point is the experience of a young teacher from Minnesota. His whole career apparently was devoted to painting. What he needed was some experience in the practical arts and the crafts, not more painting.

After you have secured sufficient background in your area of the arts, then production is the watchword. If you hope to be a painter you must paint; this is true in the other areas likewise. An art teacher, as has been pointed out, is like a two-headed calf—one head teacher and the other head artist. To take care of the artist part you must practice your craft. Part of each week must be put aside for this practice. Try to work out some sort of schedule for the week so that you can accomplish this. Perhaps you might be only a weekend painter,

Time for creative endeavor is a necessity if you are to continue to be of use as a teacher. An art teacher must be a professional person as well as a creative artist in some medium.

but that's better than nothing. Or perhaps it might even have to be postponed to the summer.

A professor, and painter, on the staff of a Southern college tries to spend six hours a day in his studio painting. While he is married and the father of four children, he seldom sees them because of his six hours a day in the studio. Perhaps this is carrying the practice of painting a bit too far for the art teacher, but the example indicates the urgency with which one professional person paints. And so it is with many in the art fields.

In connection with the practice of your particular craft, one must consider the subject of exhibiting professionally as an evidence of creative growth. The young person still in school or just recently graduated is at the bottom of the ladder and has his whole professional reputation to build.

To such a person one must say that you should enter every local "show" possible. Then as you gain experience enter area shows and finally national exhibitions. Enter work which you personally feel to be your best. Don't be discouraged when your work is rejected; we have all gotten rejection slips on occasion. Dig in, do a better job, and try again. Organizations quite often have listings of local exhibits in their newsletters. Professional as well as generalized publications have regular listings of area and national shows where all artists can exhibit. When entering shows one must consider costs—entry fees, shipping costs, and crating costs. But if you can win a cash award once in a while, you will at least make enough to pay expenses.

Summary

In this chapter we have discussed the problem of professional and creative growth. Under the heading of professional growth we have considered graduate work, attendance at and participation in professional meetings, professional reading, other teaching assignments, and professional writing. As to creative growth we have considered further study in the art fields, practice in the art fields, and exhibitions. These are just a few of the possibilities available for providing growth as a teacher and artist.

For Further Reading

Douglas, Harl and Mills, Hubert H., *Teaching in High School,* New York: The Ronald Press Company, 1948.

Gray, Wellington B., *A Study of Graduate Art Education,* unpublished doctoral dissertation, New York University, 1954.

Reed, Carl, *Early Adolescent Art Education,* Peoria: Chas. A. Bennett Co., Inc., 1957.

Youch, Wilber A., and others, *The Beginning Teacher,* New York: Henry Holt & Co., Inc., 1955.

For Further Thinking and Doing

1. Outline in detail a plan for your own professional growth.

2. Prepare a time budget which will enable you to devote part of each week to your own creative growth.

3. Make an inventory of the professional committees of teachers in your school and indicate the purpose and accomplishments of each one.

Professional Ethics

As in most professions, the profession of education has a code of ethics which is for the guidance of those actively engaged in teaching and allied fields. A code of ethics is nothing more than a statement of professionalism covering the actions of teachers. In reality there is more than one code of ethics; most state organizations have codes as do the national associations.

Taylor says: "Professional ethics is not like the measles. We know little of its onset, the mode of transmission, the period of incubation, the time of greatest communicability, and the methods of control. It is a condition which we *hope* is highly contagious among student teachers."[1]

Place of Professional Ethics

Probably the most extensive effort for professional ethics codification has been made by the National Education Association. Not only has this organization devised the most widely used code, but it has also done a tremendous amount of research on the ethics question. Along with this major effort has gone the investigation and statement of the various state and local education associations, and in part, the more specialized groups not connected with the National Education Association such as the American Association of University Professors.

Within the teaching profession there are those who state that professional ethics can and should be taught as course material. And there are also those who maintain that professional ethics is a state of the mind and cannot be taught as a course but must be "caught."

As a result of this kind of honest disagreement in the profession, you might or might not have come into direct contact with the area of professional ethics. But, while you might not have had a course in such an area, you have no doubt been exposed to living examples of at least the mode of professional

[1] William S. Taylor, *Professional Ethics in the Preparation of Teachers* (Washington, D. C.: National Education Association, 1949), p. 4.

123

ethics. Your professors in methods courses, the director of the placement bureau, the professor who had you make all those observation reports, were all indicating to you some of the instances of professional ethics. Whether formal course or not, professional ethics is an area in which you must be interested as an undergraduate and as a student teacher. In education as in other professions, the stronger the ethics practiced by teachers, the more professional becomes the job of teaching, the better the job of teaching is done, and the better children and the community are served.

But how do you handle the ethics question when you are a student teacher? You will be acting as a professional person when you are assigned as a student teacher. To a limited degree you will have most of the responsibilities of the regular teacher who is under contract to teach. Douglas states that codes of ethics for teachers are classified into "six areas of teacher relationships: 1) to the pupil, 2) to other teachers, 3) to the community, 4) to the profession, 5) to the administrative officers, and 6) to the board of education."[2] You can easily see that you as a student teacher will have some relationship to most if not all of these six areas, some limited and some almost vicarious.

As a student teacher you will begin to practice ethical conduct as a result of observing how things are done in your school. You will soon learn that certain relationships exist between student and teacher, between teacher and teacher, and so forth. How you make assignments, how you grade student work, the "chain of command" are all areas in which you must conduct yourself properly and in which you will certainly participate.

Historical Status

Because of a legitimate pride in their work and an inherent loyalty, teachers have banded together in the formulation of statements of recognized standards of professional conduct. The earliest statement was proposed by Georgia teachers in 1896. But in spite of this relatively early start, which pre-dates the codes of professional ethics of the American Bar Association (1908)[3] and the American Medical Association (1912)[4], the widespread current interest in professional ethics is a recent movement in education. Probably this is due to a rebirth of the pride which teachers traditionally have in their work and the fact that teachers have just begun to awaken to the whole problem of professionalism.

[2] Harl Douglas and Hubert H. Mills, *Teaching in High School* (New York: The Ronald Press Company, 1948), pp. 586-587.

[3] Professional Ethics Committee, *1947 Report* (Washington, D. C.: National Education Association, 1947), p. 53.

[4] *Ibid.,* p. 45.

The National Education Association appointed its first committee on ethics in 1924. As a result of the work of this committee, the first code of the association was adopted in 1929 and the revised version in 1941.

The most unique feature of the codes which have been adopted by state associations, as well as the National Association, is that the enforcement of the points covered in the codes is essentially voluntary and must be observed more by persuasion than by compulsion.

Code of Ethics

As previously mentioned, the National Education Association has done a tremendous amount of work in the field. While the complete text of its official code covers several pages, a condensed version printed several years ago in the Association's *Journal* covers the main points of emphasis to be found in many codes of professional ethics for teachers.

A Code of Ethics[5]

The teacher should be courteous, just, and professional in all relationships.

Desirable ethical standards require cordial relations between teacher and pupil, home and school.

The conduct of the teacher should conform to the accepted patterns of behavior of the most wholesome members of the community.

The teacher should strive to improve educational practice through study, travel, and experimentation.

Unfavorable criticism of associates should be avoided except when made to proper officials.

Testimonials regarding the teacher should be truthful and confidential.

Membership and active participation in local, state, and national associations are expected.

The teacher should avoid all indorsements of educational materials for personal gain.

Great care should be taken by the teacher to avoid interference between other teachers and pupils.

Fair salary schedules should be sought and when established carefully upheld by all professionals.

No teacher should knowingly underbid a rival for a position.

[5] National Education Association, "Ethics for Teachers: A Condensed Statement of the Code of National Education Association," *Journal of the National Education Association*, XXXIII, p. 117.

No teacher should accept compensation for helping another teacher get a position or promotion.

Honorable contracts, when signed, should be respected by both parties and dissolved only by mutual consent.

Official business should be transacted only through properly designated officials.

The responsibility for reporting all matters harmful to the welfare of the school rests upon each teacher.

Professional growth should be stimulated through suitable recognition and promotion within the ranks.

Unethical practices should be reported to local, state, or national commissions on ethics.

The term "teacher" as used herein includes all persons directly engaged in educational work.

Bill of Rights[8]

Douglas states that codes of ethics are usually in the negative, they stress the "don't" aspects of ethics.[6] He also says that perhaps the profession needs to take a positive stand on some of the issues important to the profession.[7]

In 1947, apparently feeling a need for this same kind of statement, Schorling composed his *Bill of Rights for Teachers.* In spite of conditions in the public schools, particularly in post-war America, and in many cases continuing into the present with more severity, Shorling had the courage to state what was at the time the unattainable. His statement follows:

BILL OF RIGHTS

1. The right to teach classes that are not too large—in general from ten to twenty.
2. The right to have time in the school day for planning.
3. The right to a 45 hour week.
4. The right to adequate compensation for the full year of fifty-two weeks.
5. The right to an adequate amount of helpful and constructive supervision.
6. The right to have good materials and enough of them.

[6] Douglas, *op. cit.,* p. 588.

[7] *Loc. cit.*

[8] Raleigh Schorling, "A Bill of Rights for Teachers," *Journal of the National Education Association* (November, 1946), p. 478.

7. The right to work in a room that, with the help of the students, can be made pleasant and appropriate to the tasks to be learned.

8. The right to the same personal liberties which other respectable citizens assume for themselves as a matter of course.

9. The right to an internship.

10. The right to a realistic program of in-service education.

11. The right to participate in modifying the curriculum and methods.

12. The right to keep from being lost in the profession.

While it is most important to attempt to achieve the pinnacle of perfection in terms of professional conduct, it is also important for the public to understand the "rights" which a teacher can reasonably expect. Perhaps in these days of overcrowded classrooms, inadequate supplies and equipment, and the apathy of the community, Schorling might seem farfetched in his statement of the rights of teachers. But one must again have the ideal toward which to strive. Situations are never going to improve until someone makes the effort. Perhaps you will see the day when the "rights" expressed and others that shall be added will become realities.

Summary

The National Education Association gives the best possible example of the Utopia in ethical conduct. Those teachers who subscribe to and follow the Code are the ones who are the most professional minded teachers that we have. This Code, and others which are similar, actually offer guideposts to a professional way of life that we should all practice and protect.

While you may not have been exposed to a college course called "Professional Ethics," you now have the opportunity, as a student teacher, to observe examples in your daily contact with other teachers and to practice the examples which you see.

Men, being human, have found such Codes a necessity for daily practice in their profession just as the Golden Rule is the basis for ethical living to the layman in his daily personal life.

Lastly, mention was made of the responsibility which the community has to the teacher in terms of the statement of a "Bill of Rights." While some of the items listed in the example given are years away, one must strive for that which is best for the child as well as the teacher.

For Further Reading

Douglas, Harl and Mills, Hubert H., *Teaching in High School*, New York: The Ronald Press Company, 1948.

Professional Ethics Commission, *1947 Report,* Washington, D. C.: National Education Association, 1947.

National Education Association, "Ethics for Teachers: A Condensed Statement of the Code of the National Education Association," *Journal of the National Education Association,* XXXIII, p. 117.

Schorling, Raleigh, "A Bill of Rights for Teachers," *Journal of the National Education Association* (November, 1946), p. 478.

Taylor, William S., *Professional Ethics in the Preparation of Teachers,* Washington, D. C.: National Education Association, 1949.

For Further Thinking and Doing

1. Participate in a panel discussion on the importance of professional ethics.
2. Collect statements of professional ethics from state and local teachers' groups. Notice the frequency of statement of certain of the enunciated principles.

Securing a Teaching Position

THERE are many avenues through which one can secure a teaching position. These avenues include the college and university placement bureaus, commercial teachers' agencies, personal contacts, notices in professional journals, and placement opportunities as advertised in other sources, including the newspapers.

College Bureaus

Your Alma Mater undoubtedly has a placement agency which helps place graduates of the institution in teaching positions. As soon as you are definitely sure that you want an art teaching position, register with this placement bureau. Usually there is no charge for this service. "Most beginning teachers secure their first positions through the cooperation of their own training institutions."[1] The Director or his agent will probably want to interview you to determine the kind of position you wish, the location you prefer, and the level of instruction for which you feel best suited. Besides securing certain kinds of information from you, the interview provides an opportunity to explain how the placement bureau works, and gives the one doing the interviewing a chance to "size you up" as to personality.

Photograph

Quite often you are requested to provide a photograph for the placement service to use in recommending you to prospective employers. There are some states, notably New York and Pennsylvania, which have employment regulations which *prohibit* the use of photographs by employment agencies for the purposes of fair employment practices. However, if you are able to use a photograph, you will find that it can be of great help to you. You should choose a photo which really looks like you. Don't provide the Hollywood type of glamor photo. Remember that the school superintendent is trying to hire a teacher—he

[1] Harold Spears, *Principles of Teaching* (New York: Prentice-Hall, Inc., 1951), p. 224.

isn't casting a floor show. This means that you should be wearing conservative clothing; have your hair fixed as you usually wear it; avoid dramatic lighting, over make-up, and an excess of jewelry. Choose a picture which shows you to advantage and one which indicates your personality. Many times the college annual is an excellent source for the original photograph. Wallet-size photographs are generally the most acceptable. The placement office can usually suggest several firms which can furnish you a number of copies of your photograph at a modest cost. "Since superintendents tend to make an original selection of the candidates they would like to interview on the basis of the paper qualifications, the photograph plays an important part in determining whether you will be one of those chosen."[2]

References

There is little doubt but that you will be asked to furnish references. While the practice differs from place to place, it is usual to provide forms on which these references are to be submitted. Ethics call for these references to be submitted directly to the placement bureau or to the person or persons to whom your application is submitted—you do not handle them; they are confidential material.

It is wise to have all of your reference letters located in one spot. Since the first contact in seeking a position is usually through the college placement office, it is advisable to have all available references filed with this office.

There is always a big question in the minds of most beginners as to whom one should ask for references. A very simple rule to follow is to choose people who can do you some good. "If there is any doubt about the willingness of the person to whom he would refer to give him a very favorable recommendation, he should not list that individual's name," say Douglas and Mills.[3] Choose people who can speak about you from firsthand knowledge, people who know you personally. If possible, select several people from your college art department, professors who have had you in studio classes and who know of your creative ability. Include names of teachers under whom you have done your student teaching. The latter suggestion is made as these are the people who have seen you perform at your best—and your worst. Submit the names of former employers, people who can speak of your ability in another field, i.e., camp directors, playground supervisors, scout commissioners, those associated with the little league movement, and foremen of commercial and industrial

[2] Wilber A. Youch and others, *The Beginning Teacher* (New York: Henry Holt & Co., Inc., 1955), p. 51.

[3] Harl Douglas and Hubert H. Mills, *Teaching in High School* (New York: The Ronald Press Company, 1948), p. 528.

concerns in which you have worked. It is advisable to submit the name of someone who can attest to your character and personal habits. It is suggested that for this purpose you submit the name of your minister, priest, or rabbi. If you are or have been a member of a regular congregation, whom better could you offer to speak on your behalf?

You should provide from six to eight references. From a number less than six the prospective employer possibly might not get a good cross section of opinion concerning your worth as a prospective teacher. More than eight references to check becomes a burden on the school administrator who has to do the checking.

Before you submit the name of anyone as a reference, always ask permission to use the person's name. This is nothing more than common courtesy.

Application

Usually a placement bureau will send you a notice when a position is reported. When you receive such a notice, be businesslike and answer immediately whether or not you are interested. If you are not interested, this position can then be mentioned to another likely candidate. If you are interested in the position, write a letter of application to the person or persons mentioned in the original notice you received from the placement agency. If there is no name mentioned, address your letter to the superintendent of schools. Of necessity this is a business letter and not a friendly letter.

A letter of application is usually your introduction to the prospective employer. You should state your interest in the position available and mention your qualifications as clearly, specifically, and concisely as possible. One way to do this is by means of the "data sheet." The data sheet (so-called by many institutions) is a prepared outline giving pertinent information of a personal nature, i.e., address, weight, marital status, and so forth; educational preparation; teaching experience; other work experience; military service; and a list of references. An example of this type of "data sheet" is to be found on pages 132 and 133. The more complete the information is, the longer the data sheet is. Give as complete information as possible, but make the results as short as possible—one to two pages. The data sheet is not a substitute for the letter of application. It tends to make the letter of application shorter and more personal. See the Appendix for an example of a letter of application.

Interview

If, after receiving your letter, the prospective employer is interested in your services, he will more than likely wish an interview. Such an interview is just as advantageous to you as it is to the employer.

PERSONAL DATA SHEET

NAME   John J. Smith

ADDRESS   505 Sunset Street
                Jarvis, Penna.

TELEPHONE   Jarvis 3140

AGE   24

WEIGHT   165 lbs.

HEIGHT   5'8"

```
                                              ┌──────────────┐
                                              │              │
                                              │  PHOTOGRAPH  │
                                              │ (If permitted│
                                              │  by law)     │
                                              │              │
                                              └──────────────┘
```

EDUCATION

Jarvis High School, Jarvis, Penna. Graduated June 1952.
Central State College, Center City, N. Y. Graduated May, 1958,
        Bachelor of Science in Art Education. Major: Fine Arts
        Minor: English.
New York University, New York, N. Y. Summer school, 1956.
Art Students League, New York, N. Y. 1952-53. Professional
        courses in painting with Eric Ryan.

TEACHING EXPERIENCE

One semester of student teaching in elementary and high school,
        Center City public schools, Center City, N. Y.
Summer camp counselor in arts and crafts, Camp Upton, N. Y., 1954.

OTHER WORK EXPERIENCE

Clerk, Sun Drug Co., Center City, N. Y. Part time for two years.
Baby sitter. Part time while in high school.

MILITARY EXPERIENCE

Two years in U. S. Army Reserve, rank of corporal.

PROFESSIONAL ACTIVITIES

Educational: Panel member at state education meetings.

Art   : One-man shows in Center City and Jarvis.
              Worked as a manufacturer of costume jewelry.

Memberships: Eastern Arts Association, American Federation of
              Artists, Delta Phi Delta.

- 2 -

REFERENCES

Dr. J. A. Gone, Chairman, Art Department, Central State College,
    Center City, N. Y.

Prof. H. A. Smith, Art Department, Central State College, Center
    City, N. Y.

Miss May Joiner, Critic Teacher, Jones School, Center City, N. Y.

Hugh R. Brown, Manager, Sun Drug Co., Center City, N. Y.

James L. Barrett, Director, Camp Upton, N. Y.

1st Lt. James Boyd, Commanding Officer, Battery "B", 347 F. A. Bn.,
    Center City, N. Y.

Rev. Arthur Wallace, Minister, First Methodist Church, Jarvis,
    Penna.

The interview gives the school superintendent a chance to "size you up" as a potential member of his faculty. He wants to see how you look, hear how you speak, and ask questions to determine how you think and what you know. "In the interview, the applicant should permit the employing official to determine the course and scope of the interview and to do most of the talking and questioning."[4]

This meeting will give you an opportunity to visit the community and see the place where you might be employed. You will also have the opportunity to meet the people with whom you will work (particularly the administrators) and to ask specific questions concerning the terms of your employment, which can best be answered face to face rather than by letter. Matters of salary, methods of payment of salary, tenure, extra-curricular activities you would be responsible for supervising, class load, and other such matters are appropriate for discussion at a meeting of this kind.

It is to your advantage to find out all you can about the community and the school system in which you are interested prior to arriving in the community. In many cases, the placement service on your campus can give you much valuable information about the community and the school situation. Personal friends who might live in the community, fellow students who have attended schools in the community, the Chamber of Commerce, and even your church minister, priest, or rabbi can be helpful in supplying or securing information for you.

Often it is advantageous to take along some samples of your own work so that the school authorities may see what you can do yourself as a creative individual. If the material you would like to take is too large for convenience in handling, 2"x2" colored slides of the work can be good substitutes if the slides themselves are done in a professional manner to show your work off to the best possible advantage.

Always carry an extra set of your qualifications, i.e., the data sheet, to leave with the school authorities in case they have lost or misplaced the one set sent to them or in case they have need for another set for their own purposes. Should you have to leave this material with them, be sure that it is professional in appearance; that is, be sure that the pages are not dog-eared, that they are clean, and that they are enclosed in a binder or folder of some kind. A regular term paper binder, such as the kind most colleges have in their book stores, is adequate.

Be sure that you are neat, clean, and professional in appearance. Dress is most important. Dress conservatively without too much jewelry. Don't overdo the paint, lipstick and bright nail polish, the loud ties and socks. Look like a business man or woman.

[4] Douglas, *op. cit.*, p. 526.

There are several rules to follow in the actual interview which will make for more pleasant relationships all the way around. The first is punctuality. Be on time. If the appointment is for 2:00 P.M., be there just a bit before that time so that you will not keep a busy school executive waiting and waste his valuable time. If there are forms to fill out, do it cheerfully. Many administrators have their own forms that they feel are necessary.

When you meet the superintendent, the principal, or the committee which is going to do the interviewing, be friendly and courteous. Get to the point of the interview as soon as you can but let the person or persons conducting the interview take the lead in making the first move in any direction. Answer questions fully and as concisely as possible. Volunteer the fact that you have brought some of your own work with you (or slides, as the case may be) and that you would be happy to have them see the work if they would care to take the time. If they would like to see the work, *you* take it from the portfolio (or hand them the slides) piece by piece and right side up. Explain what it is that they are looking at as you hand them each separate piece. However, do not monopolize the conversation; say enough for the explanation and let it go at that.

Never apologize for your work or your ideas at such a meeting. It's too late for this now if apologies are necessary. You've got to sink or swim with what you have, not what you might have brought with you.

When the question of salary comes up, discuss it frankly. After all, it's your life and living that you are bargaining for. Be firm if asked what salary you expect. A statement, such as "I feel my services are worth $4500 for the school year," is ample. You should investigate the salary schedule to determine what you can expect prior to going to the interview. Some states have state salary schedules; all teachers with the same degree, preparation, and experience start at the same salary step on the schedule. It is sometimes wise to let the administrator tell you the established salary for the particular position and for one of your background before you make a statement. Always be sure that transportation is covered in the salary or in some other way if you will be required to travel from school to school. Some schools have supplementary contracts for such activities as coaching, sponsoring the yearbook and/or newspaper, teaching adult classes, and so forth.

Above all, don't wear out your welcome in the interview. When all the points considered important by all parties have been covered sufficiently and you sense that the time has come to close the interview, gather up your materials, bid goodbye, and leave, making certain that you shall hear from the administration one way or another concerning the position on a mutually acceptable date.

When this date has come and you receive word from the superintendent that you will be employed if you are still available, be sure that you contact him immediately, regardless of the answer that you will give. If the answer is affirmative, sign the contract if one is enclosed and if it states what you have agreed to previously. Now is the time to cancel all other possible commitments regarding employment.

Contract

In public school situations your name must be presented to the local school board for approval before you can be employed. Should you be approved by the board you will then have a position and will be a member of the teaching staff. Some school districts offer contracts; others do not. Most districts offer contracts for a period of one year when a contract enters the picture at all. This contract will state the conditions of employment for the teacher. Some states regulate the terms and kinds of contracts offered; this is especially true in states where there are tenure laws. In most instances involving tenure, the contract is made for a period of one year and can be renewed yearly until such time as tenure status is achieved. As an example, teachers in Pennsylvania achieve tenure status at the beginning of the third year of "successful" teaching experience. In districts in Illinois having tenure for the system, the state requires certain requisites be met for continued year to year certification. While this is not a tenure regulation per se, it most certainly determines whether or not the teacher is certified to teach for the following year. If he is not certified, he cannot teach, and therefore, has no tenure.

There are districts which do not offer contracts to their professional employees. If this is the case in the district in which you are interested, it is suggested that you secure a statement in letter form of the employment and employment conditions to which you have agreed. This letter should be signed by the secretary of the local school board, showing that this action is official. In most instances, such a letter has legal standing, and it is to your advantage to have as much legal protection as possible. "Since a beginning teacher can hardly be expected to know all the statutory regulations pertaining to employment, it is best to ask for a written statement of employment."[5]

The contract should be clearly specific as to 1) the amount and payment of salary and 2) the teaching assignment. "All other provisions, such as requirements to swear loyalty to the Constitution, or to refrain from teaching certain doctrines, should be looked upon with suspicion, as should provisions relative to community duties, place of living, membership in organizations, or any other restriction of *any* type on the full rights and privileges of a free citizen."[6]

[5] Spears, *op. cit.*, p. 231.
[6] Douglas, *op. cit.*, p. 532.

Commercial Teacher Agencies

The commercial teachers' agencies have perhaps placed millions of teachers since they first began operations. Some are of national scope, while others serve particular areas. In times past, many college professors of education have thought that association with such an agency was not professional, was in poor taste, and was just not the proper thing to do. Contrary to these thoughts, commercial placement agencies for teachers have fulfilled their mission in placing teachers in positions of their choosing in sections of the country which could not be covered in other ways. By and large, these agencies are run by competent professional people, many of whom are former teachers and administrators. To maintain the best of practices, many of them have banded together and have organized into the National Association of Teachers' Agencies.

The commercial agency has placed many a teacher in a position at some distance from his college or university because of the wide coverage of available positions which the agency lists. This would be an almost impossible feat for the smaller college placement bureau. These agencies usually charge a small registration fee which covers the cost of setting up your file in their office. Should you accept a teaching position as a result of a notice from an agency, you will probably be expected to pay a commission for the work the agency has done in your behalf. Normally the commission charged is five per cent of your first year's salary. Many agencies arrange payment over a period of time during the first year of teaching. Special arrangements can usually be made. It is possible that you will belong to several agencies at the same time. There are times when several of these agencies will send you a notice of one particular position. It is sometimes difficult to decide which agency to do business with when this happens. Usually you deal with the agency whose notice of the available position you received first. Be sure to notify the other agencies that you have applied for the position through another source. Be sure to keep copies of *all* correspondence with agencies and school administrations for your own protection.

"The private agency has certain advantages of which you should be aware:

1. The private agency has greater effectiveness . . . when jobs are scarce.
2. When the desired position is out of the 'service area' of the college, the private agency is likely to have more influence.
3. The private agency is likely to place more emphasis upon the matter of salary."[7]

A list of the members of the National Association of Teachers' Agencies can be found in the Appendix.

[7] Youch, *op. cit.*, p. 61.

Certification

The college or university from which you are graduated cannot provide you with a license to teach. This is the prerogative of the state education department in the state in which you are interested in teaching. It is the responsibility of this department to see that all art teachers meet the minimum standards of preparation as set up by the particular state. Sometimes the college will provide forms for the state in which the college is located, which when completed, are forwarded to the state education department requesting a teaching certificate.

Direct application (together with an official transcript of your college work sent by your college) should be made to the state education department of another state when you are interested in a different area of the country.

Little has been written specifically about certification for art teachers. Perhaps the most recent complete study was done by Beelke in which he deals directly with certification requirements for teachers in art.[8]

Professional Journals

Often, professional journals carry notices of available teaching positions. These professional publications include state school journals, certain art publications, and several specialized journals, such as that of the American Association of University Professors. On occasion publications, such as *Arts and Architecture* and *American Artist,* have carried advertisements concerning position vacancies.

Other Sources

Other sources from which information can be secured concerning available positions are large metropolitan newspapers and your friends. Private schools, particularly, advertise in the press. Quite often friends know of your availability and will recommend you for a position or will mention the position to you for your action. Strange as it may seem, there are times when your present superintendent (if you are an experienced art teacher) will recommend you for a better position even at the risk of losing you himself.

Another way to learn of available art positions is to write letters of inquiry to school superintendents in areas in which you are interested. In such a letter you inquire as to the availability of an art teaching position in his schools.[9] It is always wise to include a stamped self-addressed envelope for the convenience of the superintendent—you are more likely to receive an answer

[8] Ralph G. Beelke, "A Study of Certification Requirements for Teachers of Art in the United States," *Research in Art Education* (Kutztown: National Art Education Association, 1954), pp. 28-77.

[9] Youch, *op. cit.,* pp. 61-62.

in this way. If you write a letter of inquiry, just ask if there is or will be a position available in art. If you hear that something will be available, then you can make formal application. An example of a letter of inquiry is to be found in the Appendix.

A final way in which to learn of possible positions is to check with your major professors, particularly your department chairman or dean. These people quite often are asked by administrators and teachers in the field to recommend art teachers. Many times these positions are not formally listed in the placement office on campus and are mentioned to the professors in confidence. Keep in touch with your department, let the professors know that you are looking for a position and what it is you would be interested in specifically.

Summary

In this chapter a number of possible sources of information concerning available positions in art teaching have been explored and techniques as to your conduct in some of these situations have been covered.

Sources of position information include: the college placement bureau, the commercial teachers' agency, the letter of inquiry, professional and commercial journals and the press, friends, and the college art faculty.

The technique of the interview, the contract, certification, references, the photograph, and the application have been discussed in some detail.

The ways mentioned in this chapter have proven quite effective in dozens of cases in numerous school systems throughout the United States. They are mostly step by step procedures which are a "must" from a professional point of view in securing a teaching position. The superintendent and the school board expect the information and expect that the routine will be performed in a uniform manner. Youch lists in question form a number of points to be considered as "The Mechanics of Finding a Job."[10] Such a checklist might prove helpful to you in your search for a teaching position.

For Further Reading

Beelke, Ralph G., "A Study of Certification Requirements for Teachers of Art in the United States," *Research in Art Education*, Kutztown: National Art Education Association, 1954.

Douglas, Harl, and Mills, Hubert H., *Teaching in High School*, New York: The Ronald Press Company, 1948.

Spears, Harold, *Principles of Teaching*, New York: Prentice-Hall, Inc., 1951.

[10] *Ibid.,* pp. 55-58.

Youch, Wilbur A., and others, *The Beginning Teacher,* New York: Henry Holt & Co., Inc., 1955.

For Further Thinking and Doing

1. Write a letter of inquiry for a specific position. Write a letter of application.
2. Construct a personal data sheet for use in applying for an art teaching position.
3. Make a list of all possible sources of information concerning positions available in art teaching.

Appendices

APPENDIX I

National Association of Teachers Agencies[1]

ARIZONA
>Arizona Teacher Placement Agency, 1540 W. Jefferson, Phoenix

CALIFORNIA
>Southwestern Teachers Agency, 405 Citizens National Bank Bldg., 453 S. Spring St., Los Angeles

CONNECTICUT
>Cary Teachers' Agency, 49 Pearl St., Hartford 3

DISTRICT OF COLUMBIA
>Adams Teachers Agency, Colorado Bldg., 14th and G Sts., N.W.

ILLINOIS
>Albert Teachers' Agency, 37 S. Wabash Ave., Chicago 3
>Clark-Brewer Teachers Agency, 64 E. Jackson Blvd., Chicago 4
>American College Bureau and Yates-Fisk Teachers Agency, 28 E. Jackson Blvd., Chicago 4
>Hughes Teachers' Agency, 25 E. Jackson Blvd., Chicago 4
>Illiana Teachers Service, 4th and Green Sts., Champaign

IOWA
>Clinton Teachers Agency, 706 S. 4th St., Clinton
>Edwards Teachers Agency, 224 Insurance Exchange Bldg., Sioux City 13
>Sabins Educational Exchange and Midland Schools Teachers Agency, 202 Shops Bldg., Des Moines

MAINE
>New England Teachers' Agency, 407 Libby Bldg., 10 Congress Sq., Portland 3

MARYLAND
>Baltimore Teachers' Agency, 516 N. Charles St., Baltimore 1

MASSACHUSETTS
>Grace M. Abbott Teachers' Agency, 120 Boylston St., Boston 16
>Cary Teachers' Agency of Boston, 120 Boylston St., Boston 16
>Fisk Teachers' Agency, 120 Boylston St., Boston 16
>New England State Teachers Agency, 120 Boylston St., Boston 16
>Mildred Baldes Teachers Agency, 120 Boylston St., Boston 16

MICHIGAN
>Detroit Teachers Agency, Park Avenue Bldg., Detroit 26
>United Teachers Agency, 201 Main St., City Bldg., East Jordan

[1] Help in compiling this listing was given by Mr. Paul Albert, Albert Teachers' Agency, 37 S. Wabash Ave., Chicago 3, Illinois.

MINNESOTA

Clark-Brewer Teachers' Agency, Rand Tower, Minneapolis 2
Educational Service Bureau, 1133 Plymouth Bldg., Minneapolis 3
Minnesota Teachers Service, 800 Plymouth Bldg., Minneapolis 3
Schummers Educational Service, 4532 France Ave., Minneapolis
Western Teachers Exchange, 215 Plymouth Bldg., Minneapolis 3

MISSOURI

Clark-Brewer Teachers Agency, 1028 Dierks Bldg., Kansas City 6
Specialists' Educational Bureau, 508 N. Grand Blvd., St. Louis 3
Wood Teachers Agency, 804 Grand Ave. Bldg., Kansas City 6

MONTANA

E. L. Huff Teachers' Agency, 2120 Gerald Ave., Missoula

NEBRASKA

Davis School Service, 528 Stuart Bldg., Lincoln

NEW JERSEY

Strahan Teachers Agency, Hotel Stacy-Trent, Trenton 8

NEW MEXICO

Southwest Teachers' Agency, 1303 Central Ave., N. E., Albuquerque

NEW YORK

American and Foreign Teachers' Agency, 551 5th Ave., New York 17
Associated Teachers Agency, 522 5th Ave., New York 36
Bardeen-Union Teachers' Agency, 316 S. Warren St., Syracuse 2
Clark-Brewer Teachers' Agency, Flatiron Bldg., New York 10
Cooperative Teachers Agency, 47 W. Huron St., Buffalo 2
Dorothy Madder Teachers Agency, 342 Madison Avenue, New York 17
Eastern Teachers' Agency, 288 Sunrise Highway, Rockville Centre
Educational Placements, 516 5th Ave., New York 36
Interstate Teachers Agency, 82 St. Paul St., Rochester 4
Kellogg Teachers' Agency, 31 Union Square, New York 3
Pratt Teachers' Agency, 33 W. 42nd St., New York 36
Private School and College Bureau, 30 E. 39th St., New York 16
Schermerhorn Teachers' Agency, 366 5th Ave., New York 1

NORTH DAKOTA

Midwest Teachers Service, 314½ DeMers Ave., Grand Forks

OHIO

Northern Teachers Agency, 1836 Euclid, Cleveland 15
Central States Teachers and Professional Agency and Advisory Service, 710
    N. Clinton St., Defiance
Teachers Placement Bureau, 50 W. Broad St., Columbus 15

OREGON

Northwest Teachers Agency, 1101 Loyalty Bldg., Portland 4

PENNSYLVANIA
Bryant Teachers Bureau, 1025 Witherspoon Bldg., Philadelphia 7
Great American Teachers' Agency, 205 N. 7th St., Allentown
Central Teachers' Agency, 202 Walnut St., Harrisburg
Horning Teachers Agency, Devon
Pittsburgh Teachers Bureau, 944 Union Trust Bldg., Pittsburgh 19

SOUTH CAROLINA
Southern Teachers' Agency, 1420 Henderson Street, Box 364, Columbia

TENNESSEE
College and Specialist Bureau and Southern Teachers Agency, 502 Goodwin
    Institute Bldg., Memphis 3
National Teacher Placement Service, Box 309, Chattanooga

TEXAS
Southwestern Teachers Agency, Stephanville

VIRGINIA
Southern Teachers' Agency, Broad-Grace Arcade, Richmond

WASHINGTON
Clark-Brewer Teachers' Agency, 505 Columbia Bldg., Spokane 8

APPENDIX II

Student Teacher Rating Form[1]

EDINBORO STATE TEACHERS COLLEGE
EDINBORO, PENNSYLVANIA
Student Teachers Rating Form

Name_____ Subject or Grade_____

Critic _____ School_____

Tentative Ratings on _____ Date_____

Ratings should be checked in accordance with instructions found in the Manual for Student Teachers.

	A B C D F
Directness and clearness of aim	_ _ _ _ _
Ability to plan	_ _ _ _ _
Versatility with subject matter	_ _ _ _ _
Success in motivating work	_ _ _ _ _
Clearness in expression and illustration	_ _ _ _ _
Skill in eliciting and directing discussion	_ _ _ _ _
Care of individual differences	_ _ _ _ _
Evaluation of pupil achievement	_ _ _ _ _
Efficient use of class time	_ _ _ _ _
Wholesome pupil-teacher relationship	_ _ _ _ _
Discipline	_ _ _ _ _
Classroom management	_ _ _ _ _
Efficient use of instructional materials	_ _ _ _ _
Effective use of physical equipment	_ _ _ _ _
Appearance	_ _ _ _ _
Speech	_ _ _ _ _
Enthusiasm and initiative	_ _ _ _ _
Responsibility	_ _ _ _ _
Cooperation	_ _ _ _ _
Emotional maturity	_ _ _ _ _
Command of English	_ _ _ _ _
Breadth of scholarship	_ _ _ _ _
Professional attitude	_ _ _ _ _
Leadership	_ _ _ _ _
Participation in out-of-class activities	_ _ _ _ _

Recommendations: Estimated Evaluation _ _ _ _ _

[1] State Teachers College, Edinboro, Pennsylvania.

146

APPENDIX III

Final Estimate of Teaching Ability[1]

FORM TPB-13. 6-27-52-6M (1A-1882)

FINAL ESTIMATE OF TEACHING ABILITY — 6

PERSONAL

	Unsatisfactory	Poor	Good	Very Good	Superior
1. English usage	☐	☐	☐	☐	☐
2. Voice and speech	☐	☐	☐	☐	☐
3. Physical appearance	☐	☐	☐	☐	☐
4. Poise	☐	☐	☐	☐	☐
5. Emotional stability	☐	☐	☐	☐	☐
6. Sense of humor	☐	☐	☐	☐	☐
7. Friendliness	☐	☐	☐	☐	☐
8. Courtesy	☐	☐	☐	☐	☐
9. Promptness	☐	☐	☐	☐	☐
10. Reliability	☐	☐	☐	☐	☐
11. Forcefulness	☐	☐	☐	☐	☐
12. Open-mindedness	☐	☐	☐	☐	☐
13. Judgment	☐	☐	☐	☐	☐
14. Cooperation	☐	☐	☐	☐	☐
15. Industry	☐	☐	☐	☐	☐
16. Adaptability	☐	☐	☐	☐	☐
17. Originality	☐	☐	☐	☐	☐
18. Versatility	☐	☐	☐	☐	☐

PROFESSIONAL

	Unsatisfactory	Poor	Good	Very Good	Superior
19. Subject matter	☐	☐	☐	☐	☐
20. Accuracy	☐	☐	☐	☐	☐
21. Methods	☐	☐	☐	☐	☐
22. Planning	☐	☐	☐	☐	☐
23. Presentation	☐	☐	☐	☐	☐
24. Questioning	☐	☐	☐	☐	☐
25. Professional ethics	☐	☐	☐	☐	☐
26. Leadership	☐	☐	☐	☐	☐
27. Use of available material	☐	☐	☐	☐	☐
28. Understanding of students	☐	☐	☐	☐	☐
29. Attention to individuals	☐	☐	☐	☐	☐
30. Ability to inspire confidence	☐	☐	☐	☐	☐
31. Enthusiasm	☐	☐	☐	☐	☐
32. Ability to discipline	☐	☐	☐	☐	☐
33. Ability to stimulate	☐	☐	☐	☐	☐
34. Ability to make adjustments	☐	☐	☐	☐	☐

Name ....
(First)   (Middle)   (Last)

Subjects ....

School ....

Inclusive dates ....

to ....

RECOMMENDED

NOT RECOMMENDED

OTHER

(Line out what does not apply)

35. (A *brief* personal statement of the kind which will help a prospective employer)

36. I think this candidate gives promise of becoming a:

☐ unsatisfactory ☐ poor ☐ good ☐ very good ☐ superior teacher.

....**Supervisor**

STATE UNIVERSITY OF NEW YORK
NEW YORK STATE COLLEGE FOR TEACHERS
Albany

[1] State University of New York, New York State College for Teachers, Albany, New York.

APPENDIX IV

Confidential Report on Teaching[1]

FORM S. T. 104

OFFICE OF STUDENT TEACHING
East Carolina College
Greenville, N. C.

Grade _____

CONFIDENTIAL REPORT on the student teaching of _____
                                                                    (Name)

Grade (or subject) taught _____ School _____

Personal Appearance:

Personality:

Scholarship:

Teaching Technique:

Work Habits:

Class Control:

Language Habits:

Professional Attitude:

Remarks:

Fall ☐
Wtr. ☐
Spr. ☐   _____   _____   _____
              (Date)   (Supervising teacher)   (Supervisor)

OWEN G. DUNN CO., 97080

[1] East Carolina College, Greenville, North Carolina.

148

APPENDIX V

Letter of Inquiry

1508 East Fourth Street
Greenville, North Carolina
January 8, 1960

Dr. John P. Jones
Shippingport Public Schools
Shippingport, Virginia

Dear Dr. Jones:

On May 18 I will graduate from East Carolina College, Greenville, North Carolina, with a Bachelor of Science degree. My major is in art education.

I wish to locate in the vicinity of Shippingport so that I may continue my education at the University of Virginia. For this reason I am writing you to find out whether there will be a position available in art education beginning in September, 1960.

If such a position is available, I would like to make an official application. My thanks for your consideration.

Sincerely yours,

Robert L. Williams

Robert L. Williams

APPENDIX VI

Letter of Application

1508 East Fourth Street
Greenville, North Carolina
January 15, 1960

Dr. John P. Jones
Superintendent of Schools
Shippingport, Virginia

Dear Dr. Jones:

My thanks for your letter of January 11 giving me information about the position of supervisor of art, which will be available in September. Please consider this letter as my formal application for the position.

I am enclosing a copy of my Personal Data Sheet which will give you rather detailed information about my background, my education, and my experience.

I feel that I am especially well qualified for the position of art supervisor because of my education and my experience as art director for Camp Short, North Carolina.

I shall be available at your convenience for an interview, should you desire to talk to me in person.

After you have had an opportunity to read over my papers, I would appreciate hearing from you concerning my application.

Sincerely yours,

Robert L. Williams
Robert L. Williams

Index